Christopher Gale
Forest Resources & Environmental Science
Michigan Tech University
1400 Townsend Dr.
Houghton, MI 49931-1295

Secrets of Major Gift Fund Raising

By
Charles F. Mai

The Taft Group • Rockville, Maryland

SECRETS OF MAJOR GIFT FUND RAISING

Printed in the United States of America

91 7 6 5 4 3

LIBRARY OF CONGRESS
Library of Congress Cataloging-in-Publication Data

Mai, Charles F.
Secrets of major gift fund raising / by Charles F. Mai.
p. cm.
Bibliography: p.
ISBN 0-914756-39-7
1. Fund raising. I. Title.
HG177.M35 1987
658.1'5224—dc 19 87-25568
CIP

The Taft Group is the nation's leading publisher and information service organization serving the needs of nonprofit organizations and institutions.

The Taft Group • 12300 Twinbrook Parkway, Suite 450 • Rockville MD 20852
(800) 877-TAFT (301) 816-0210

Dedication

To Betty, Nancy, and Chuck for their help, love, and encouragement.

TABLE OF CONTENTS

LIST OF FIGURES

ACKNOWLEDGMENTS

This book is based primarily on columns which have appeared since 1985 in *Fund Raising Management* magazine as "Cultivating Major Gifts." The magazine is edited by William Olcott and is published monthly by Hoke Communications, Inc. at 224 Seventh Street, Garden City, New York 11530-5726. Thank you, Bill, for your encouragement in many ways. My neighbor and friend, Dr. Seymour Smith, former president of Stephens College, has kindly given me ideas for columns.

Thanks to Kenneth Miller of Columbia, Missouri, and his expertise from the years at the University of Missouri for suggesting the book and for his guidance.

I owe the greatest debt to my daughter, Nancy Kreighbaum, to my wife, Betty, and to my son, Charles Jr., for editorial and typing help.

Special appreciation goes for the gracious and informative letters from Philip Menninger and from Patrick Burnau of The Menninger Foundation giving permission to quote Philip Menninger, Dr. William Menninger, and Dr. Karl Menninger.

Special thanks to David Sharpe, Director of Professional Books and Vice President of Operations, The Taft Group, who did far more work personally on my manuscript than I thought editors ever did. David, you are a patient man.

PREFACE

The people I admire most in development have worked for an excellent institution for *many* years and have developed the art of making friends of donors. One important gift follows another year after year, then charitable remainder trusts and an important bequest. Those achievers find great pleasure and deep satisfaction in their jobs.

Most of us fall short of that ideal, but these stories will help point the way.

Chapter 1

MAKE IT REAL—PART ONE

Yes, there are donors who respond purely to the dollars and cents attraction of the big gift, and yes, you must always keep the tax advantages in mind. But the majority of large gifts I have seen made were given because the gift was more than money—it was a gift of life, of education, of research, of gratitude, or any of the many different things that give meaning to our existence.

I believe that the successful fund raisers I have known were successful for the same reason. Their jobs were more than jobs or a salary—they were opportunities to joyfully experience life, and these fund raisers succeeded in communicating that joy to the people they met. They developed relationships and showed concern. They saw their prospects and donors as individuals with human needs. Above all else, they made what they did real, to themselves and to their prospects. And all involved were the better for it.

This is why I begin and end this book with chapters exhorting you to remember why we as fund raisers do what we do. In an age of increasing economic pressures on the nonprofit institutions and organizations we work for, it becomes easier to see the cold dollar quotas and five-year plans than to see the warm, living, and breathing reasons for our quest.

Fortunately, those reasons are always close by, and we need only look around to be reminded of them. Remember them, as do I and countless of your colleagues, and you will do well.

* * *

I went into development in middle-life and found it fascinating and fun to learn. Presentations on behalf of a school and organizing people to raise money were activities similar to the selling and sales management of my previous jobs. The product was different but the techniques similar. I had had experience in putting up a new building so I felt at home in two major areas of work. My biggest thrills came from new experiences. Two days after I started I was asked to join our president and dean in a conference with Dr. Lovinger, a visiting college president. This meeting was a review of our total educational effort. It gave me a tremendous thrill to deal with such challenging and basic problems.

* * *

"Please talk to my mother about your college." That was from a high school student who was so anxious for an art education but afraid her parents could not be persuaded. It was a pleasure to help with the persuasion.

One of the minor joys was to again participate in the relaxed business lunch. The subjects discussed at these luncheons included art appreciation seminars, fund-raising efforts of other colleges, the function of design in business, etc.

* * *

The public relations area was especially fascinating. I talked to radio-TV personalities Walt Bodine and Jean Glenn about their program "Conversation," had the fun of seeing several of our stories featured on the front page, and enjoyed comparing notes with professionals like Jim McQueen. In meeting Vincent Price at the airport, I found him a warm, relaxed person. Senator Stuart Symington and his gracious wife spent a pleasant hour in our president's office discussing art after a ground-breaking ceremony.

* * *

The biggest thrill of all was to watch the Student Living Center rise. Something like this complex of two dormitories, art gallery, cafeteria, lounge, and library had been long hoped for. I had the good fortune to arrive when things were right to accomplish this major improvement—energetic president, forward-looking board, etc.

On other campuses, I found complaints about student apathy. Not here. These design and fine arts students were here for what they wanted most—development of artistic skill. The inspiration for a college comes from its students and I really found incentive here to help these young people get a fine, well-rounded education.

I understood what it all meant the day the freshmen arrived on campus. Everything new to them, those eager faces full of hope—Adventure, Achievement Ahead! I was glad to have a way to help them, even if indirectly.

Work, at a college, is still work. Figures have to be added, letters written, calls planned, meetings conducted—the same as in business. The means of accomplishment—in terms of equipment such as typewriters, filing cabinets, and office machines—are similar except that they may not be as good. Nor does the difference lie in the sweep of grass and shubbery outside the windows. The campus is part of the delightful environment, but incidental. The main thing is work in the most vital area of life—education. All achievements have resulted from some type of education. A share in a great task is a spring of vitality and happiness.

I did not choose fund raising because it was a high calling or could lead to great rewards. It was simply work I was qualified for, enjoyed, and felt to be worthwhile public service. It is one way to be a generalist in this age of specialization. I have found many ways to apply my wide range of business and academic experience.

As for joy in the work, the best was to know many wonderful people and to share with donors the thrill of great achievement in their gifts.

When I think of the fascinating people I have enjoyed, one who comes first to mind I never did meet.

A board member told me he knew Bob Hope and would arrange a meeting so I could invite him to campus for a benefit. On two California trips, this was scheduled. But it didn't work out. I never had an answer to my letters or phone calls.

One day a sophomore drama student asked me, "Would you like Bob Hope to do a benefit here? He will pay his own expenses." I replied with an amazed, "Yes, how did you manage that?" She told of playing in a summer theatre where he appeared and she asked him directly. She said, "Just call his agent, set the time, and he will come." It took me only a few minutes to arrange everything. I was amazed but the student was absolutely confident it would work fine.

It did go to the board for routine approval where a member brought up a question, "Won't Hope draw a big crowd? and won't people tramp down the grass?"

That did it. We had to phone the agent and try rather unsuccessfully to explain why we could not invite Bob Hope to campus. He did come to our town the day specified and gave a benefit for another institution.

Of course, this board decision was not just a case of giving undue importance to the grass (which already had a lot of weeds). The board wanted to project an image for the school of serious academic achievement and *that only.* A noble ideal. But they might have been well advised to listen to students and prospective students. Another instance that it is best to assign primary importance to the individual (or customer, as it would have been in my IBM days).

* * *

Another man I only saw a few times: once when happy and prosperous and last when rich and miserable. I handed him the means of saving his life, but he did not act on it.

This was a dentist near Orlando, Florida. He enjoyed a flourishing practice, civic leadership, delightful family, and, especially, his orange grove. Every weekend he worked among his trees and it was his pride and pleasure. A truly happy man!

Disaster came in an unlikely form: the development of Disney World. They wanted his orange grove and began making a new and better offer each week. The dentist was overwhelmed with the offer of riches (which he didn't need).

Salvation appeared as a unitrust. I explained how he could give the land to his daughter's college, enjoy a lifetime income, a big charitable deduction, and get rid of his problem. The trustee agreed to sell the land to Disney World. When the dentist and his daughter died, the money would go to improve education at the college.

Actually, he did not sell or sign the unitrust—he died of a heart attack—immobilized by the illusion of sudden wealth.

* * *

Finally, I'm aware customs and attitudes in various parts of the country are interesting, to say the least. I am reading James A. Michener's novel *Texas* and was reminded of a trip to Austin.

At the airport an alumna met me in a huge, black limousine, which she drove herself. "This was L.B.J.'s." We then drove to the Texas Supreme Court to meet the judge. He said, "I'll drive you home for dinner." I wondered what kind of vehicle her husband would have. How could anything surpass a presidential limousine? It was a full-size truck. The chief justice explained that his hobby was cutting down trees and he needed the truck to haul logs. He was summoned from miles around to take down difficult trees and needed to be fully equipped. These two were great fun. They had the money and the daring to do what they wanted to do. May you approach fund raising with as much daring.

Chapter 2

CULTIVATE, MOTIVATE, ASK, AND FOLLOW UP

Much has been written about how to identify prospects, but precious little exists on what to do after you have found your prospect and are in a face-to-face situation. Time and time again I have seen good prospects lost because those involved either didn't know what to do, how to do it, or when to do it. Even though prospect development is nothing more than the social art of applied friendship, it is one of the most difficult of them all. Keep this in mind as you read this chapter and relive some of my more humbling experiences.

THE TWO DRIVING FORCES

In different kinds of interviews I have finally learned: Simplify. Be Direct. Come to the Point.

At the same time I believe most strongly in long-range cultivation. This involves doing lots of things to help the donor and generates ever-increasing gifts.

How do those goals go together? The first means be honest in stating your purpose, which is to find financial support for your institution.

The second means that it may take you years to develop the big outright gifts, trusts, and bequests you hope for.

You must educate those who believe that bequests and other big gifts come in by themselves, "over the transom." There is always a history of cultivation, of effective interviews, behind every major gift.

At Baker University, I opened the mail one morning to find a check for $100,000 from an attorney handling an estate. I didn't recognize the name of the testator and found nothing in our files. We were happy but mystified.

A year later, the daughter of a former president visited the campus and asked, as we walked around the grounds, "Did you ever get anything from Mrs. ________?" My reply, "Yes, we received a $100,000 bequest a year ago."

"Wonderful! I am so glad. Daddy went to see her many times and she often stayed with us. He hoped so much she would do something big for the college."

Excellent interviews paid off again in a long-range plan.

Big gifts start small. A story is told about Country Day School in Kansas City. The committee identified the best prospect for a building campaign. His two sons had graduated and it was thought he would give out of his great resources in their names.

Three important board members were selected to make this call for the largest kickoff gift. The prospect listened with interest, got his checkbook and handed over a check for $25.

The board members said, "Thank you," smiled weakly, and left thinking they had failed. Not so.

The prospect came to watch construction and to study the plans. Then he mailed a check for $50,000.

After more questions and observation, a check followed for $100,000. Eventually he became the largest contributor in the campaign, exactly as projected.

CULTIVATE

The following story of a major gift cultivation demonstrates the power of *motivation* once it is offered a channel of expression.

Cultivation of major gifts often takes many months and sometimes years with progress interrupted by difficulties and unexpected developments. However, this experience illustrates one time everything went right.

Twice I was faced with the option of spending an entire day in travel for a fifteen-minute interview. In addition, other time—consuming trips were taken with no assurance of any benefit. I asked myself, is it worth such an investment in time and money? Yes, because when your board finance committee wavers in support of your travel expenses, it helps to have this type of story to tell.

Dr. Jones was a county doctor during the Great Depression in the Bootheel of Missouri when his brother decided one afternoon to check the fishing possibilities. He went out in the country and was looking at the fish in the stream from a bridge on a little-traveled road. Suddenly the brother decided to see how the fish were on the other side of the pool below the bridge. Wrong timing!

A car sped along at that moment and killed him. The brother had taken out a $10,000 life insurance policy payable to Dr. Jones, double indemnity. The local judge told me, "You could just about buy the county in those days for $20,000," and that is what the good doctor started to do. He had the money-making touch. And was not unmindful of philanthropy.

Every year, when the United Fund came around, he reached into his pocket to find a $1 or even a $5 bill and seldom asked for change.

Giving to his wife's college was, of course, not to be considered. But his wife thought of it, and soon after he died she sent $1,000 without being solicited. The small school did not receive many unexpected gifts of such size, so I started asking around and discovered she had a cousin who was also an alumna and was active in alumnae leadership.

She provided background information including the fact that the father of one of our students lived in the same small town in southern Missouri and knew Mrs. Jones well. My plan was to find out if Mrs. Jones would be willing to fund an infirmary on the campus of her alma mater. The parent advised talking to her lawyer first and emphasized the importance of clearing everything with him. The father arranged for the three of us to have lunch at the Country Club and the lawyer approved my plan.

Seeing Mrs. Jones herself proved very difficult. She was quite ill; did not like to receive strangers and did not want to get dressed because she felt her appearance was poor due to her illness. She refused to make an appointment. I thought the only choice I had was to drop in and hope for the best. Before we tried that, though, my friend suggested I see her son.

Her only living child was an eye doctor in Virginia. He agreed by phone to a fifteen-minute interview at noon (he said he never took time for lunch anyhow). That was another long trip, but I arrived at his office just before noon. He listened politely to my presentation of the proposed building, but made no response other than, "Your time is up."

All was ready now for the attempt to see Mrs. Jones. My friend took me to her house and she was luckily just coming out the door to go to her P.E.O. meeting. This meant it was one of her better days and she was already dressed for company. She agreed to listen to us for ten minutes, otherwise she would be late.

I laid a rendering of the proposed infirmary on the porch table and described the main features. She looked at me with hostility and said, "I know what you want—you are asking me to give to this building. I already gave $1,000 to my school and that is enough."

I replied, "No, we want you to donate the whole building and to name it." The next eight minutes went by in silence and I worried that my friend would say something to break her thought process while she looked at the plans. Finally she said, "We will name it for my family." She was thinking of her father, who was the college doctor for many years, and of her uncle, husband, and son—all physicians, all interested in her college.

Late that afternoon she phoned and told us that her attorney and her son both approved the major gift in the name of the family.

MOTIVATE

Have the right words ready. This experience shows the importance of advance preparation, especially of having the right words to say at the crucial point. Notice that I did not make a big pitch on this project. I showed her, graphically, a way to do what *she* wanted, something big for her college and for her family. Her son and his family were already well provided for and Mrs. Jones had no desire to spend large sums on herself. She was strongly motivated to accomplish something significant with part of her money. I found, with help from friends and relatives, a project which appealed to her.

When dedication time came, I phoned and invited her to attend but she said I should ask her son. He said, "Sorry, too many commitments." When I called back to tell her, she replied, "Call him again in ten minutes." This time he said, "Sure, I'll come."

The dedication was a great day and I gave her a photo album which included pictures of her son giving his speech, the crowd and the main features of the building—especially the furnishings given by her cousin. This time I was invited into her parlor for a relaxed visit and her pleasure was a great satisfaction to me.

The first time I saw Mrs. Jones she was so ill that she was thought to be dying, hardly ever stepped outside the house. Her husband had never imagined that she would outlive him. But the idea of building her own infirmary on her own college campus, dedicated to the cause of medicine, sparked a new life in her. This gift appeared to give her new vitality and joy in living. A major gift is good medicine for the donor.

Search for the motivation. Sometimes motivation is difficult to determine. For example, we needed some money to improve journalism teaching at Baker University. I remembered that a publisher in Topeka had given us a used printing press which performed very well and that he had contributed heavily to the Journalism School of the University of Kansas.

Based on motivation assumed from those facts, I prepared a proposal on our journalism plans and went over it with him in his newspaper office. His reaction, "Why should I help you compete with my K.U. Journalism School?"

Several calls on the same prospect can help. I then asked President William Scarborough to go with me to present other gift ideas. We could not determine if any appealed to him. So I kept trying.

I discovered that the father of one of our students played golf with the publisher and asked our parent to make an approach for a gift. He did.

Then I found an alumnus in Independence, Missouri who knew the daughter of our prospect well. As a result of his request, the daughter talked to her father.

I talked to two of the publisher's top executives.

I was surprised one day to find a check for $8,000 from the prospect. Why did he send it? He never gave me a hint, although I saw him several times after that happy event. So don't worry if you never discover the true motivation. (Just worry if you don't get the check).

One thing is certain. Several approaches to the same prospect helped (I think).

On an annual campaign, we discovered that the card of a very important prospect was still on the table. Jim had decided to make the call, but did not tell anyone, pick up the card or report on his call. So another volunteer went on the call and was told "Oh yes, Jim was in last week on that and I told him I could not handle any more gifts this year. How many years have I given?" "Nine." "Well, I don't want to break my record, I will write you a check for $1,000."

Bring out the motivation. A little special attention may be what it takes to spark motivation. Someone gave us the address in Rockford, Illinois of a "lost alumna." She had been missing from our rolls for many years and had heard nothing from her college. I phoned to say how glad we were to have found her and she sent a check for $1,000. Then I visited with her and her husband at her home, enjoyed lunch with her at the Women's Club and both visited our campus. After that came a check for $10,000. Why did she send those gifts? I didn't find out, but should have. Our long-range cultivation plan for her got lost in the press of other duties. If a little personal attention did that much—think what more might have done.

Concentrate on the donor's cause-related needs. Be sure you can recognize whether the motivation is related to your charitable purposes—and what to do when it is not.

I went to New York City to make some calls and found eight inches of snow. Fortunately I could walk to all my appointments and had a pleasant, warm hotel as refuge from the sharp winds blowing the snow.

As usual, in addition to scheduled meetings and interviews, I had phone calls to make. One of these was to an alumna in Connecticut. She said firmly, "I want you to come up tomorrow night for dinner at 6:00 P.M. My husband and I want to talk with you." I felt like saying, "But that means I will have to rent a car, drive into areas I have never seen and try to get back into Manhattan after dark—and I was hoping to see a play." Instead, I said, "Thanks, I will be glad to come."

After careful study of the Hertz maps and some luck in getting through the snow accumulations, I arrived at exactly 6:00 P.M. Wonderful!

Almost before saying hello, the alumna whispered, "We want to talk to you about our wills." Drinks, a good dinner, and idle conversation went on until 10:00 P.M. when I mentioned that perhaps I should be starting back. Her husband responded, "We want to talk to you about our wills." Then he described his in detail. She also described her will completely.

I listened carefully, but could think of no helpful comments, since they had taken care of everything just as they wished.

All this time each talked only to me and offered no comments on what the other said. Afterward, she told me that neither had any idea that the other even had a will.

I contributed nothing except to be the means of their discussing a difficult subject.

What motivation did this evening uncover for giving to the college? None. But I felt the trip was worthwhile just as a service.

Sometimes we can be helpful without regard for gifts. However, I did not make a followup.

Did I ever get back to my cozy motel room? Yes, but signs were snow-covered and hard to see at night. Getting lost in the New York area on a stormy night is not recommended.

Recognize the individual. Be careful about appealing to the desire for recognition. Be subtle. But use it to offer your donor maximum gift satisfaction. It took me a while to understand how this works.

An important donor and board member handed me a check for $10,000 with this statement, "I want this to be absolutely anonymous." At the next board meeting, I read the names of recent donors with amounts. Bill said, "You left out my gift of $10,000." So, I learned that "anonymous" has various shades of meaning.

I asked an alumna to give $150 for a seat in our new auditorium and mentioned the nice brass plate with her name. She replied, "I will write you a check for $150, but we do not care about a brass plate. We do not like to see our name in public."

I knew she didn't really mean exactly what she said. So, with a little persuasion, she gave me the names to engrave. There were so many I had to have a special plate made. Several months later, she stormed into my office, "You spelled my mother's middle name wrong." So, I learned how important recognition is, no matter what the donor says in the beginning.

Learn and listen. Read the literature on motivation. In *Communication Briefings,* volume 5, number 4, the top four interests of older Americans are stated by Sandra Bunnell:

1. Health (includes safety and crime)
2. Financial Security
3. Closer Relationship to God
4. Closer Relationship to Family

Stanford Magazine for spring 1986, describes "The Stanford/ Harvard Survey" which "explores the views, values and self—images of alumni." Whether or not you graduated from Stanford or Harvard, many of your big gift prospects have similar attitudes. See things from their viewpoint in your search for motivation.

You can sound out motivation by creating giving clubs, memorials, proposals, recognition events, etc. Mostly, *listen* to the prospect. What is important to him? It may take many calls and letters and much gathering of background information.

Making "The Call"

Sometimes a volunteer hesitates to make an important call to begin, or to take another step, in the cultivation of a major gift. Why? The reason may be simple: he is unsure of what to say. The solution: give him some words.

Establish rapport. Start the interview with encouraging personal or business comments to establish a pleasant rapport: "Your son Tom played a great game on Saturday," or "That was an interesting story about your company in the paper."

Our local paper sometimes has to dig hard for feature stories. As a result, it has done one on me. Even though reporters spoke with people who know me well, the story came out O.K. While I pretended not to be excited, I was amazed at how delighted I became each time someone mentioned the story. Look for a similar icebreaker, then quickly turn to business: "How do you *feel* about the cancer problem?" Then listen—I mean *really* listen—with full attention. You will hear about the beloved sister who died of cancer and the close friend who lost an only child. With motivation identified, you are likely to have a major gift prospect.

Use emotion wisely. Invite emotional rather than merely intellectual response. Emotion powers big gifts. If you ask, "What do you *think* about cancer?" a well-informed prospect may recite lots of facts about the disease that reveal nothing about his willingness to face separation from substantial property.

It may work out better to first ask questions about your cause rather than about your organization. If your cause means a lot to him, then go on to ask how he feels about your group. If your goals have strong pull, you can build on them to kindle enthusiasm about your specific projects. Have your annual report, fact sheet and specific folders available to answer questions quickly.

Focus on the prospect. All through this discussion, you will be looking for areas of special interest, and for additional motivations to contribute. Find those compelling incentives that will make the prospect want to donate gifts *and time.* Greater participation means greater future gift possibilities.

Focus on what the prospect needs. My excitement about the largest gift commitment I ever received was quickly killed.

Having spoken with one of the richest men in the United States many times over the years and with his friends and associates, I finally discovered one strong philanthropic interest: research and treatment for the diseases and problems of old age. He was able and willing to give millions.

When I announced the good news to the president of our organization, he was disappointed in me. "Charlie, didn't you read the list, approved by the board, of what purposes we want to raise money for?" "Yes," I replied, "but—" He interrupted, "Go back and ask your prospect to make his gift to an approved program! Anyway, we are just about to drop our small department of geriatrics."

I did not go back. I knew it was of no use. The prospect put the money into his two foundations, which are now among the major foundations of the United States.

I think the president was wrong to focus on only what *he* wanted. In this case, the prospect's objective was a good one that should have been considered. The ensuing years saw fast growth in geriatrics; we missed an opportunity to expand facilities to world leadership in a major field.

But you may have a case where the donor's motivation needs guidance from you.

Help your prospect make a good gift. There are times when it is our responsibility to persuade the prospect to review some facts. I received a note from a Kansas City attorney that one of his clients had named her alma mater, Columbia College, in her will. On my next trip to Kansas City, I went to the attorney's office to thank him and he mentioned that the bequest was restricted. It was for construction of a dormitory for which she designated a name. We had just completed a dormitory and had no need for another. There were no funds to maintain a useless structure and no place to put one. I began asking questions. This was a thirty-year-old, single, schoolteacher, with no means except a car and a modest savings account. If she were to die soon, she would not leave enough to start a dormitory, even if we could think of a reason to build one. But, her attorney told me, she expected to inherit substantial property from relatives. She might have $500,000 to $1 million for this unfortunate project.

I obtained the attorney's permission to call on the woman to suggest a change to "general purposes of the college." She agreed in ten minutes. Incidentally, attorneys are usually more secretive. It was fortunate that this one sensed the need for a change in wording.

* * *

I had no idea of how to open or of what to discuss when I called on the president of an insurance company in Akron. He was an impressive man who had headed all kinds of fund drives and was the father of a prominent alumna. As an insurance man, he had extensive knowledge of estate planning. As a guiding spirit of university drives, community funds, hospital campaigns and so forth, he knew every way to make a gift, I thought.

After some comments about progress at Stephens College, I mentioned some trust plans with special emphasis on how a grandfather could provide for grandchildren with a charitable remainder term trust. I selected this because his son-in-law was a successful surgeon and I believed the only relatives he felt any need to provide for were his four grandchildren (against future possible disaster). The twenty-year term trust for grandchildren as a class and discretion reserved to the trustee captured his interest. He said, "I have never heard of this and it is exactly what I need to learn about." It proved once again that every person of means needs to know more about charitable trusts. The many interesting possibilities of trusts often make a good opening to a major gift discussion. A short, easy-to-read folder on each kind of trust is available from Philanthropy Tax Institute, Sharpe, Newkirk and others listed in the Appendix.

The folder or brochure as technique. To make it easy for the volunteer to get started, show him how to use a folder as a track to run on. He can underline certain points and discuss these with the prospect. If he doesn't get the check on the first call, he can leave the folder and return for it with the purpose of getting the check then. In a long cultivation, this can be repeated with new folders and brochures in a continuing education process.

Most important in building confidence for an effective call is to have plenty of background information about the prospect. Encourage him to tell you what he knows about your cause and your organization. Find out where he is—where you must start from. Keep a few good selling points firmly in mind to introduce at appropriate times.

Have a closing ready. If you intend to ask for the gift on this call, do so. However, if this is just a step in the cultivation process, select your final words in advance. End the interview in a way that leads to the next level, such as: "I will phone you next Wednesday to hear your thoughts on this proposal and to set a time for our next meeting."

The Importance Of Friendship

If my brother were starting a career in major fund raising, and I tried to give my best advice in just six words, they would consist of: "Be a Friend to Your Prospect." Nothing else is so important.

A great friend makes a great fund raiser. I spent years competing with Dr. M. Graham Clark, long-time president and now chairman of the board emeritus of The School of the Ozarks. I lost to him so many times in seeking major gifts that it was very educational for me and a pleasure to work with him in recent years when he became volunteer chairman of Planned Giving and Legacies for the American Cancer Society, Missouri Division.

I have also been present several times when he was with his own donors. They are not prospects to Graham Clark but friends. He loves them, enjoys them—and they love him. He gives steak dinners, country breakfasts, fruit cakes, products of the mill, calendars, pens, and all kinds of presents to his supporters and finds great enjoyment in being with them.

The largest gift in the history of the American Cancer Society, Missouri Division, was obtained by Clark in the form of a trust. It was embarrassing that our biggest gift was just 5 percent of the total he obtained. The testamentary trust amounted to so many millions that all of the several beneficiaries were astounded at the sums received.

The donor of this trust was difficult and did not like to be asked for gifts to charity. He almost threw Clark out on the first call, but the president of this mountain school persisted and eventually they became close friends. During the last weeks of the donor's life, Clark drove across Missouri to visit his friend in the hospital every week, even in the worst winter weather. Clark proved his friendship and won the full trust of the donor to help plan disposition of his fortune. The president of Washington University said to Clark in the hospital one stormy day, "Do you guard him every minute?" Clark replied, "I have to with people like you around."

Another great fund raiser. Graham Clark reminds me of the late Dr. Will Menninger, long-time president and a founder of The Menninger Foundation. He and Graham are the two greatest fund raisers I have met. Graham and Will had no trouble getting appointments. They were showered with invitations for themselves and for their wives. They hardly had to ask for gifts, because everyone wanted to help. When it became known that Will liked to collect stamps, he was given so many that stamps became the largest item in his estate. Will received gifts in such abundance in those years that The Menninger Foundation Board was faced each year with the question of what to do with the surplus. These were two sincere and loving friends to their donors.

Be a friend because you want to be. Helene Brown, American Cancer Society volunteer, tells an impressive story of how she developed a major gift.

A man walked into an office of the Society, and asked, "How much salary does your executive vice-president for California make?" No one knew and the receptionist was about to brush off this elderly man with the strange question, when Helene said, "Let me talk with him." They went into a private office and Helene offered to obtain answers to his questions. He lived in a nearby hotel and there were no hints as to whether or not he might be wealthy or important.

Helene went to great lengths to answer his many questions. For example, when he asked about research, she did not just hand him a list full of scientific terms. She wrote or visited the scientists to obtain descriptions in ordinary English.

During several meetings in his hotel lobby, they became friends. Finally, she asked what he planned to do for the work of the Society. He replied, "I will name you in my will." She responded, "We cannot be satisfied with that. The cause of fighting cancer is so important, we must ask you to designate the American Cancer Society as the sole beneficiary of your estate, since you have no individuals you wish to benefit." He agreed, "You are right. All of the data you have given me is convincing evidence I should give everything to the cancer cause."

Helene had no idea of the size of his estate, so she was astounded when he died a few months later and she found her friendship to a lonely old man resulted in the largest gift the Society had ever received, over $11 million.

How does your prospect see you? Sometimes we may not realize that the prospect has reason to see us in the opposite way—as unfriendly, not interested. When I started to work at a college, I found that an alumna living in California was recorded as having named the college in her will. I noted her as one to see on my next trip to her area. But that was not to be.

When I phoned her and asked for an appointment she replied, "Why call me?" I said I wanted to describe programs at her school and tell what is going on today. "Not interested, but I want to know how you got my name and why you called." So I was backed to the wall and told her what the records showed. "Oh, that was fifteen years ago and I have heard nothing since. Now I have other interests and have changed my will. Don't bother to contact me again." Cultivation of a major gift has to be planned and continued over the years. Fast turnover of development people is part of the problem in carrying this out. An average tenure of 2½ years is not enough. Many times a former employer has publicized a major gift which I had worked on years before and wondered if anyone was carrying out the long-range cultivation I had in mind.

What is important to your prospect? One of the first lessons in how genuine expressions of friendship can get results happened when I started as assistant to the president of Baker University. I drove to a small Kansas town to speak at an alumni dinner in the basement of the Methodist Church. On arrival, I discovered that the telephone committee had not yet begun to function, so I offered to do some phoning. On my first call, the lady said she would like to come but had no ride, and that she lived way out in the country. I said I would bring her and asked directions. Then I realized I had to leave immediately to make it back for the dinner. I feared the attendance might be small, but at least I would increase it by one.

Her home was lovely and surrounded by vegetable and flower gardens, lovingly cared for. In spite of wishing to hurry back, I took a few minutes to admire the plantings which she said were the special pleasure of her recently deceased husband. She enjoyed talking about the flowers and their care as we drove into town.

On our return after dinner, she handed me a $5.00 bill, "for your expenses." That was the only time I ever received a gift for development. Whenever I begin to feel too much self-importance, I remember the value she placed on my work and that others seem to value it even less.

Soon after, we had a conference on campus to plan a garden and landscaping. I, of course, was asked to provide the money. My friend in the country and the love she and her late husband had for Baker came to mind. I sent her the layout and plans and asked for $8,000. A week later, I visited her home again and she had the check ready for this memorial to her husband.

In working with a prospect, I try to listen for what is important to that person and to be helpful in any way I can as a friend.

Sometimes this effort is difficult. Then I remember the love of people so evident in Dr. Will, in Graham Clark, and in Helene Brown and how important it was in their great achievements.

Interview Tips

While at IBM, I took a course in selling at Northwestern University where I learned many methods of inducing the prospect "to buy." Examples: get background data, observe interests from photos and plaques in the office, assume acceptance (not "Will you buy?" but "Do you want one or two?" or "Where should it be delivered?"), start small and build up the power of your presentation gradually. Sometimes I tried to use these ideas, but the course was taught by a real estate man and I decided that data processing was quite different.

Then, in my training as an IBM salesman, I listened to Thomas J. Watson, Sr., often called "The World's Greatest Salesman." He more than earned that as well as other illustrious titles. He said, "Many salesmen hesitate to make a call because they do not know what to say. It's simple. Just tell about our products, what they do for our customers." Right! I did that and made the 100% Club every year.

Learn to interview for credit reports As a reporter for Dun & Bradstreet in Kentucky, Illinois, Indiana, and Michigan, I did interviews every day but never thought about techniques. All I did was identify myself and start in on the questions. With about fifteen minutes per call in those days, there was no time to think of anything fancy. If a man refused financial information, I replied, "I will report that to your creditors and insurance companies and get what estimates I can of your financial worth." Sometimes that caused them to think twice. Or, I might say, "You didn't give a statement last year either, would you like to know what I reported?" This usually resulted in corrections of net worth estimated too low.

I found the best interview was pleasant, short, and direct.

Control the interview. An extreme example makes the point. During World War II, I became a special agent in the Counter Intelligence Corps. Then I began to concentrate on interview techniques and learned the methods which later proved so effective in business, especially in selling data-processing equipment.

The problem: how to get a subject to confess? In the United

States we had time for extensive investigation of a case, to obtain evidence from a variety of sources. In combat, in Europe, I often had to decide twenty to thirty cases in a few hours since we would capture another group the next day. The only way was to have the subject confess quickly and send him off to prison or concentration camp.

I tried some elaborate methods, even some borrowed from the Gestapo. However, the most effective method was very simple. I had a secretary who was pleasant and well known in this part of Austria as the daughter of the bank president. She asked the questions and repeated the answers to me in English. Soon the subject was saying, "Tell him this but omit that, etc." He told her all the incriminating information but what she passed on to me was only that specified. I was paying little attention, even looking at papers, signing letters, etc.

Suddenly, I looked directly at the subject and repeated his confession in German. He broke down and told us anything else we wanted to know. In a few minutes he was on his way to a concentration camp across the Inn River in Germany. This trial usually took only fifteen or twenty minutes and resulted in a firm conviction with signed confession. Although I don't advocate this technique, the point is that you should control the situation or you'll never achieve your goals.

Conducting in-depth interviews. In later years I represented colleges and health organizations in talking to financial supporters about major gifts, especially by will or trust. This meant tuning in with powerful motivations—reaching deep into a person as in the Austrian and German interviews. But how to do it? I found that feelings are the important things and I should go directly to that.

I asked about cancer experiences. This would bring out a story of a relative or friend who had gone through terrible suffering with cancer—motivation established. Once a prospect told me he felt more strongly about the American Heart Association since he had lost six executives to heart attacks and none to cancer—lack of strong motivation established, find another prospect.

ASK FOR THE GIFT

Trustees of the Kansas City Art Institute were discussing how to approach Joyce Hall, founder and the head of Hallmark Cards, for a major gift to the building program. This was of great importance to the campaign, since Hall was our largest donor, both in gifts to date and in potential.

The pitfall of the ultimate plan. The chairman said, "Who should go to see Joyce Hall? Who does he respect? Who will he listen to?" One of the trustees, a key executive at Hallmark, said, "He's had business dealings with Walt Disney and admires him. If you could get Disney to approach Joyce about a big gift, he would pay attention."

Another trustee added, "Didn't Disney take some courses here at the school?" As director of development, I was handed the job of researching the Walt Disney connection.

Incidentally, one amusing aspect of this session was that the trustees decided that three carefully selected trustees should make the approach to Hall and that no one else should speak to him about a gift. They specifically instructed me not to speak to him about our campaign.

Three trustees were selected and reselected a few times, but no call was made. It was so important to do this exactly right that it was never done at all.

I was tempted to violate this prohibition several times, including one opportunity when Joyce Hall invited me to his penthouse for dinner. Another time we had a half-hour private conversation at the Kansas City Country Club and then he phoned to ask me to arrange for the president of the college to go out to his farm for a talk. Probably he was surprised that neither I nor the president or anyone ever asked him for a gift. What about the research on Disney?

Was the rumor true that Walt Disney was the best known alumnus of the Kansas City Art Institute? Disney lived his early childhood on a farm near Marceline, Missouri and was educated in Kansas City and Chicago. Before going to Hollywood, he worked in advertising drawing in Kansas City.

Although his history hinted at the possibility that he might have been a student, no proof could be found in the scanty records of those days. I even went through a boarded-up and forgotten storage room jammed full of discarded student work, hoping to find a drawing with his name on it. No luck. In fact, I found nothing of interest such as a reject from Jackson Pollock; or from his teacher, Thomas Hart Benton.

Some supporters of the Institute decided, nevertheless, to stage a gala dinner at the Kansas City Country Club to award

Disney an honorary Doctor's degree as our famous alumnus. The next question was how to get Disney to attend.

After discussing this with various groups, I discovered that one of our young volunteers and his wife were good friends with Disney's daughter and sometimes visited her. On their next trip west they extended the invitation through the daughter and it was accepted.

Disney was in an enthusiastic mood for the dinner and told of going someplace in downtown Kansas City for some art lessons, but he did not remember the name or the address. "Maybe I did go to what is now the Kansas City Art Institute. However, what I really need is not another honorary doctor's degree, but a high school diploma."

I wish I could say that Disney was asked to speak to his friend Hall and both then made large gifts. It probably would have worked, since Joyce was present at the dinner and was so happy about the occasion that he stood up and made an unscheduled speech.

However, I was leaving that same week for another position. There was no development director to encourage a followup.

The two biggest prospects were not asked for anything. Disney left money to an art institute in California and Joyce Hall's name was missing from the four buildings constructed during this campaign.

The most superb program of cultivation usually results in nothing if you stop short of asking for the gift. The magic words: "Your support is tremendously important. We need you."

Millions of dollars have been raised through imaginative cultivation such as the Disney approach, *but not without asking for the gift!*

How to ask. Is it difficult to say, "We are counting on your help," or "Your gift is vital to the opening of this campaign," or "We know your gift will inspire many others," or "Shall we put you down for the full payment now or do you wish to spread your commitment over three years?" Sometimes you may decide to mention an amount: "Some on the committee said you would give $5,000 as you did for X Hospital. However, most of us thought this project would mean so much to you that your gift might be $10,000 or more." Make it a little indirect or straight to the point, as you sense the situation. Establish in your own mind that you *will* get the gift and your confidence will have an effect on the prospect. Sales managers teach, "Assume Acceptance."

The importance of asking. When I started as director of planned giving and legacies for the American Cancer Society in Chicago, I asked my boss, Tom Baab, to arrange appointments for us with wealthy board members. The first was a leader of the Society who had held many important positions and was very dedicated. He was friendly, but two things were discouraging: 1) he paid for our lunches at the Palmer House (a tiny compensation for the disappointment he had in store for us) and 2) he spent forty minutes describing the chair he was establishing at Ohio State University through his will and by his lifetime gifts. He emphasized in detail the personal attention he had received from the president of that great university. He said nothing about any provision for the American Cancer Society, even though he knew the purpose of my being hired. Finally, I asked him straight out: "You are making a wonderful gift to your alma mater. Do you have any plans for a major gift or bequest to the Society?" He said "No" in as friendly a way as you can say that word. But we had never before asked him for a major gift. The Society sat back while his school found an appealing project and successfully presented a proposal during lunch at the president's home.

Years after the dinner for Walt Disney, when I read in the paper of Disney's bequest to the California art school, I thought, "They asked." Then I recalled the year of cultivation and the efforts of many capable people trying to achieve major gifts from the founder of Hallmark Cards and from Walt Disney. The year's work was successful in that the climaxing dinner was the most joyous and inspiring fund-raising event I ever have attended. But no one said the magic words "We count on you for an important part in our campaign." I guess that may have cost the Institute $500,000, which was twice the endowment at the time of this newly accredited college.

FOLLOW UP

Recently I spent three days with a man starting deferred gift promotion for the American Cancer Society in Missouri. I told him everything I could think of which could be important in his success.

Out of that came the realization of what I could have done better, the area where some improvement would have paid off the most: *follow up* with both prospects and with volunteers. Some examples show why you need to avoid this hidden weakness of many big gift programs.

The importance of following up. I was told that a wealthy woman in Alton, Illinois was a long-time volunteer for the American Cancer Society and had just lost her husband to cancer. I arranged a seminar in a nearby town, invited her to attend and to have dinner with me. Her neighbors brought her over for the dinner and we had a great evening making friends and discussing the charitable remainder trust idea.

Despite cold, snow and ice, the seminar on bequests and charitable trusts was well attended and enthusiasm developed. Afterward, the lady said to me, "Could I give one of my rental properties to the American Cancer Society in memory of my husband, get a charitable deduction and still have a lifetime income for myself? And could I give another house the following year? They are getting to be such a headache." Perfect!

I mailed her a proposal with copy to her lawyer who was also an American Cancer Society volunteer, and who told me he would work it all out with her. Our local staff said they would follow up. What could be better?

But Alton was a long way from my Chicago headquarters and I had no other prospects there. Nothing happened. I did send the lady two or three letters. That was not enough followup to result in action. To get that unitrust, I would have had to find time somehow to go back to Alton to talk more with the prospect and to arrange legal help for her attorney in drawing up the agreement. Lack of followup lost a series of major gifts from this fine volunteer for the cancer cause.

But here is one that I did right, at least up to a point.

Regular followup gets results. This was for the Boy Scouts. I was asked to call on a woman whose motivation and ability to give were both well established. Her late husband was an active Scout volunteer and one of the most important donors in the Council.

I went to Jefferson City about once a month on other business so began making appointments to see her every trip for several months.

This frequency of followup seemed to be about right for her. She discussed how to provide for her great-grandson, her own health, what her husband did for the Scouts, her tax situation, life insurance, etc. We became friends. I also presented her with a proposal for a $10,000 gift annuity which she liked. We arranged for her lawyer to represent her, retained a lawyer for us, and she selected an insurance company to assume the contract and the obligation of payments.

Just prior to the meeting to finalize the agreement, she said, "I would really like to give $10,000 outright to the Scouts." She also discussed doing another gift annuity the following year.

I mentioned the possibility of these two additional gifts to Pete, our executive, along with many other matters for followup in a conference prior to my retirement. I also gave the volunteer chairman information on this and other followup opportunities, some for much larger amounts. I offered to meet with his committee to work out followup details.

My suggestion was that Pete or the chairman or both visit the donor and say, "I understand from Charlie that you might consider an outright gift of $10,000 to help with the camp. Here is what the money can do. . . . The board requests your permission to name the project in memory of your husband who gave so much of his time to the camp."

Was the followup call made? I am afraid to ask, because Pete is so busy. And did she give another $10,000 the following year? Not unless she was asked. All the prospect background information, evaluation, cultivation for eight months, proposal presentation, first gift—all the time-consuming and difficult parts were done. Surely the followup will not be overlooked for such an easy and substantial gift each year.

Followup techniques. How to do followup requires careful study of each prospect. You may use phone, letter, proposal, or personal call. You may decide to ask a volunteer to help, invite the prospect to a meeting, induce involvement through service on a committee. You can find *some way* to keep advancing the sale, but you may have to stretch your imagination.

The greatest danger. The most terrible thing, the danger to always guard against, is the possibility that you might review a promising case after a year and realize no followup was done.

When I worked for Stephens College, one of our parents arranged for me to meet with his client in Sacramento who was about to sell his manufacturing business for $5 million. I estimated his capital gain to be tremendous. My friend was an investment counselor and member of our deferred gift committee. He gave me complete facts on the case and arranged the interview. The prospect showed some interest, but I decided he had no motivation to make a gift to a women's college in Missouri. However, there was reason to believe (because of his profession) that he might have a desire to support a California university where I had a friend in deferred giving, a nationally recognized expert. I turned the prospect and all the facts over to him but heard nothing. About a year later we met at a meeting and I reminded him. He replied, "Oh, I haven't had time to do anything about that yet, but it is a good idea and thank you very much." This man is highly respected with outstanding results to his credit. Even he lost a chance at a big one for lack of followup at the right time.

Ensuring your followup. "How do I keep it all straight?" you may ask. We all have trouble with this one. My suggestion is to have a large appointment book with plenty of room to write planned contacts each day and a place to put the corresponding papers needed for future calls. I use a "tickler file" for the current month and another for the next twelve months. This will tell you what you should be doing and when to focus on what is most important. On a given day you might decide to pass up a meeting to go out and try once more for a major gift. Followup should be a high priority.

But how to find the time? I suggested to my friend starting the new job that he use the phone more. Letters are necessary but usually lack power to generate action. Personal visits are often best, but budget and travel limitations must be considered. The only choice sometimes is to make most of the followups by phone.

Your friendly voice and helpful facts will advance the cultivation process more than you can believe.

Chapter 3

EXPLORE "THE RULES" FOR YOURSELF

It should go without saying that times and things change. Even so, there are the oft-stated "rules" of ours and any other game that rarely get scrutinized simply because they are the standards. You can achieve and maintain an edge in raising major gifts if you evaluate the effectiveness of these rules every so often in light of your experience, changing laws, and social custom.

TAXES AS MOTIVATOR

Be sure to cover tax aspects carefully and completely, especially in written presentations. The Tax Reform Act of 1986 increased attention to this area.

But don't emphasize tax savings. Don't present this benefit as an important motivation.

I sometimes hear the expression, "He just made that gift to pay less tax." Ridiculous! Every major gift costs $72 or $67 per $100 (depending on surtax). A gift costs $85 per $100 for lower-income donors. There is no honest way to make money by charitable gifts.

Help stamp out people saying that gifts are made for tax purposes. There was sometimes a bit of truth to that years ago, but Congress changed that.

Most large donors are very sophisticated about taxes. But not all, and there may be some misconceptions lingering from the Tax Reform Act of 1986 and from current IRS Regulations, U.S. Tax Court decisions, etc. So be sure your donor is clear on the particular items affecting his gifts.

The most basic point is that the Tax Reform Act of 1986 made no changes in the rules for itemizers. Their gifts are deductible up to 50 percent of adjusted gross income (30 percent for appreciated property).

The tax deduction for a property gift equals the fair market value. No capital gains tax. Robert F. Sharpe in *Give and Take* for October 1986 says:

> Gifts of appreciated property will grow to unprecedented proportions . . . However, a very few of these types of gifts will be subject to . . . The alternative minimum tax . . . one person in a thousand.

If appropriate, show the effect of this gift on donor's alternative minimum tax, often referred to as AMT. Susan Stern, in a *Fund Raising Management* article for November 1986, describes very well how the charitable deduction is a deduction against AMT. For a gift of appreciated property, the appreciation is included as a tax preference.

If your donor elects the 30 percent of adjusted gross income limitation of deductibility of a property gift, give the details if he will need to carry over the excess deduction for up to five succeeding years. Can the tax preference element be prorated accordingly?

A gift of tangible personal property for a use unrelated to the exempt purpose generates a deduction only for cost or tax basis.

If your donor likes to give long-term capital gain property to his private non-operating foundation, he can generally only deduct his tax cost. He should give that type of property directly to you.

Pentera (see Appendix B) calls the charitable deduction "one of the few tools left for minimizing income taxes." One example of a specific point you can emphasize is that the full fair market value of appreciated securities and real estate qualifies for the deduction. The distinction between long-term and short-term need no longer be taken into account as of January 1, 1988.

Find a good manual on the 1986 Tax Reform Act and subsequent tax developments so you can create an excellent seminar or talk at a time of great interest in tax changes. Every change is another chance for a good seminar.

Estate taxes must be viewed differently than in past years. For only the wealthy can we say, "Save estate taxes by a testamentary charitable gift." The 1981 law, which takes full effect by 1987, eliminated taxes on property passed at death for 99 percent of decedents, all those with estates under $600,000.

How can you turn tax issues into a benefit for you? Your prospect may have life insurance, purchased many years ago to pay estate taxes, which is no longer needed. Ask him to give that insurance to you. This means a charitable deduction and no more premiums for your donor.

You may have discussions with donors on providing income for children. In a custodial account for a child or children under age fourteen, unearned taxable income exceeding $500 ($1,000 if the $500 standard deduction is applied) on assets in such accounts will be taxed at the parent's marginal tax rate, rather than the child's lower tax rate.

Sharpe, in his commentary, also states that "the deferred gift plan will grow in attractiveness . . . thanks to lower interest rates and higher capital gain taxes."

The foregoing brief items are intended merely to demonstrate that you must constantly keep up with tax changes so that you can properly inform your donors. Your attorneys and other advisors are necessary and a tremendous help, but I recommend that you gradually become an expert yourself.

RULES OF THUMB—RIGHT FOR YOU?

I heard an excellent presentation in a CASE (see Appendix) meeting by a Yale development man about how to put several multimillion-dollar trusts together to form an attractive package for building construction, permanent maintenance and expanding programs. His audience was turned off. "That may be O.K. for Yale but does not apply to us." I had no immediate use for the concepts either but did apply them in later years.

The big donor. Even if, like that CASE audience, you are not working on a huge gift at the moment, I ask you to bear with me to consider why million dollar gifts are made. It may provide insight into the psychology of big donors in general. I just finished reading a 1984 book, *Mega Gifts* by Jerold Panas. It is based on indepth interviews with twenty-two donors and eight other persons, along with survey returns from one-thousand development people. The discussions covered thirty-one gifts of $1 million or more.

In this study of motivation for highest-level giving, there are some surprises.

An old rule questioned. For example, it is usual for lecturers and writers to say: "Send no more than two persons on a call." I have violated that rule a few times and was amazed with good results. The million-dollar-and-up donors selected by Panas did not mind a delegation of four or five consisting of such people as board chairman, president, the friend who made the appointment, a peer who had made a similar gift, and a staff person in charge of the project under discussion. Such a group will have complete information and enable the prospective donor to make an immediate decision in his own mind. He will later talk to his wife, attorney, etc. if he feels the final decision may be favorable. Don't worry if such a meeting takes two or three hours. This is important to the donor. John D. Rockefeller, Sr., said giving was his greatest pleasure in life. Be sure to present "bold and dramatic opportunities." Not needs, not negatives. This is your management group who must convince the donor they are successful people, capable financial managers who will carry through his important plans. He must believe in the people running your organization.

The most difficult step. Another surprise statement in the book is that "it is harder to get an appointment than it is to get the gift itself." College presidents and other CEOs have told me that the role of the development staff is to find the prospect, do the cultivation and bring the top man in only as a ceremonial gesture at the close. Panas' donors laugh at that. They say nothing will happen until they believe strongly in your mission, your board and your staff leadership. You *start* by building enthusiasm for your mission, and your president has to be part of that crucial effort. Share your vision, your dream, the excitement of the program. They want to support a cause "that has the potential for creating a significant change for good."

The value of brochures. As to those expensive, elaborate, beautiful brochures you are very proud of and which help so much in general fund raising—the really big donor says he does not like them. He hates waste of money and says those fancy productions go into the wastebasket. So, go easy on folders and brochures.

What will sell. Get him interested by volunteer participation, board membership, verbal presentations or whatever—*then* prepare a proposal *for this prospect* only. It will feature a one-page summary, supporting data, facts on your excellent financial management and necessary photographs and illustrations. You must know the prospect well enough to determine how much and what kind of detail he wants. An engineer wants blueprints, most others do not.

When the "buy" (giving) decision is made. I will mention two examples, out of my experience, which confirm the principles described in this book. One is that the decision to make a major gift is "spontaneous . . . almost an immediate spark of electricity."

Both of these gifts started with an inquiry and a phone call. I sensed, even in the first phone conversation, acceptance and eagerness to do something big. In subsequent conversations I shared their joy in making a huge gift.

The rewards of giving. Panas quotes Louise M. Davies, "I get a tremendous amount of joy out of my giving . . . that's the real payoff. It makes you glow." Such statements about the pleasure of giving are among the most significant features of the book.

Wealthy people who do not give are missing a lot of fun. How can we convince them how much giving will enrich their lives?

I took our president to have lunch with one lady at her Ohio farm home which pleased her very much. It may also have been one reason she arranged for me to go with her and her husband to her attorney's office so that she could sign the will leaving her $1.2 million farm to Stephens College.

Involve the spouse. In the previous example, I had earlier called on her husband to make sure he was agreeable. He was enthusiastic about the project, showed me his manufacturing operations, and expressed gratitude to me for finally getting his wife to make a will. He said he had been trying for twenty years to have her execute a will. Be sure to involve the spouse.

What it took to get and keep the bequest. I could not tell that any of our printed literature helped. The main factors were:

- *Renewal of loyalty.* The alumna donor visited the Stephens campus and came to believe in the mission of her college more than ever.
- *Personal visits.* I went to see her at her home and we discussed all of her plans thoroughly. I made her husband part of the project and he helped bring it to a conclusion.
- *Proposal.* I gave them everything in writing. This included tax advantages but the tax aspect was not emphasized and was of minor importance.
- *Special trip by the president.*

I do wonder what happened after I left my employment at the college. I hope she was "thanked seven times" as Panas recommends. I hope she was asked to participate in important volunteer activities such as:

- board
- alumnae organization leadership
- special committees

A bequest should be the beginning of greater participation by the donor. You must keep renewing her interest. Remember that beneficiaries can be changed and the competition is fierce.

Motivation. The other example was similar except that it was a unitrust funded by highly appreciated land. She heard me describe this type of charitable trust during her visit to the campus and that lit the spark. She was motivated in part by association with other alumnae, being part of the club, and identification with people she admired and felt close to. Then we just had to work out details about what land to use, rate, beneficiaries, etc. Most of that we did by phone and letter. She regarded this trust as the biggest achievement of her life.

They give to a dream. The facts reviewed in this book confirm what I have long suspected, that individuals "give to dreams and dazzling visions." The big gift is a great experience for the donor. It is our privilege to help make it happen and to sense the glory of giving to a large enough extent that good can be done in the world.

The million dollar gift. During my first years in the business, I did not believe anyone ever got a million dollar gift. But I finally became convinced from hearing about them at meetings and reading reports. For example, this item from the *Stanford Observer* for October 1986:

"Stanford received $179 million in gifts from private donors during the year ended August 31, 1986. This is *preliminary* to a 'major' fund raising drive in 1987."

So, what is holding you back?

Chapter 4

MAKE SPEECHES AND SEMINARS PAY OFF

When you appear before an audience which includes prospects, what can you say to stimulate thinking about big gifts?

You will describe projects, goals, costs and all the beautiful things you would do if you had the money. Fine. But what can you offer the prospective donor for himself?

WHAT TO TALK ABOUT

Try proposing the charitable remainder trust as a way for the donor to enjoy some personal benefits. It may also open thinking in the direction of big bucks. I like a human interest story as something to reach more people. Mostly, I have told true stories, even using actual names if I have permission (one more item of recognition). But if you use a made-up story, flesh it out to build interest. These are favorites which produced results.

The school teacher achieves what she never dreamed. Dorothy was a retired schoolteacher living in her own modest home, who had inherited some property from her father and was "comfortable." However,her favorite nephew was about to start to college, and she wished she could send him $500 per year as a gesture of her interest and support. But she felt she didn't have that much extra income and how in the world could she possibly earn more?

Then Dorothy remembered something. Twenty years ago her father gave her $1,000 with some financial data on various stocks and said, "Pick a good growth stock and invest the money." She chose well, since the stock increased to a market value of $10,000, but with dividends of only about $100 per year. Looking at rates advertised in the paper, she exclaimed, "If I could put that $10,000 in a bond I could have the extra $500!"

A friend reminded her that she always wanted to do more for the American Cancer Society, especially since her father had died of cancer and she had put in so many years as a volunteer. She asked the Society if anything could be done in that connection and they described the pooled fund. After checking this out with her lawyer she gave her stock to the American Cancer Society Pooled Fund. Now she gets all the interest and dividends which her shares earn in a Boston bank common fund, based on the full $10,000 market value. Her annual income has increased from $100 to over $700 per year. Not only can she send $500 to her nephew, but she has $200 to pay income tax and spend on her own pleasure! She also can deduct about $5,000 on her income tax as a charitable contribution the next time she does her income tax return.

The big thrill is that Dorothy has achieved something she never dreamed of—MADE A HUGE GIFT TO THE FIGHT AGAINST CANCER! At her death the shares in the pooled fund will go to cancer research, education, and help for patients.

A farmer finds a solution. A farmer bought his Missouri acres fifty years ago and the farm is now worth $1 million. But he is not happy! His wife died two years ago and he sold all the livestock, leaving him lonesome and with little to do. All these years he has put everything into the farm, but now with his arthritis he can do little farming and his income is limited. He doesn't feel rich at all, especially on long bitter cold nights staying alone on the farm. He is afraid to leave it unattended and he hates to sell.

Never a man to give much to charity, he nevertheless found the answer to his problem in a gift to a nearby college. By deeding over the farm to the college, he funded a trust, has a substantial income tax deduction, and will receive a lifetime income based on the full fair market value of the property. He decided on an income of $80,000 per year and took the next plane for California to visit his nephew. If he had chosen a higher amount such as $90,000 per year his income tax deduction would be correspondingly less.

Exchanging a headache for an annuity. A property investor reached the point where he was old and tired, and in looking over his holdings found he had one real headache—a large downtown building which was old, hard to rent, and needing so many repairs that some years there was no income at all. "And they talk about raising taxes still more!" Why not sell? The land was valuable and he could easily get $100,000. With a cost basis of $20,000 many years ago, that meant a gain of $80,000. What to do? His attorney said, "John, you have always wanted to do something important for your church and for various local charities. This is your opportunity. Set up an annuity trust with this and with any other properties you no longer wish to bother with and you take 8 percent of the current market value as a lifetime income, and name your wife to receive the income if she survives you." John was interested but replied that he didn't need the income and would rather provide some help toward college education for his seven grandchildren. "Fine, we will make it a twenty-year term sprinkling trust with income to the grandchildren for twenty years, then 80 percent to your church and 5 percent each to four local charities you name now or later. The trustee will have power to allocate income equally among the seven or as needed, in case one child has special requirements."

PLANNING THE SEMINAR

Now, as to seminars specifically. You must have a good list of prospect names to start with.

The local American Cancer Society office in Arlington Heights, Illinois, had built up only a few major gift prospect names. For a seminar, we remedied this lack by joining forces with a fine hospital which had an excellent prospect list. We had a good turnout in their beautiful auditorium.

I was invited to be on a panel in Kansas City where the local group failed to get out any mailing at all. They tried passing out handbills in apartments at the last minute. It was a flop and very distressing to a fine panel of speakers. A carefully prepared mailing and publicity program is essential. Don't leave home without it.

Appeal to family and personal interests. Our chairman in Springfield, Missouri, decided to have a seminar and sent out a letter which described the occasion as a fund-raising event for the American Cancer Society. The result was so negative, he cancelled. Next time, he called it "an estate planning seminar" which was successful. In fact, it attracted so much favorable attention that next year radio and TV joined in the publicity and we had an overflow crowd. All the questions were about personal estate problems, none about gifts. That is to be expected. The main benefit was that those present who saw me later *wanted* to talk to me and thought I might have some answers. Seminars are also a way to bring in new prospects and to further educate the ones you have.

Choose a location to suit your group. As to place, I have had seminars in savings and loan community rooms, churches, private homes, retirement homes, libraries, hospitals, college auditoriums, etc.

Topics for the seminar discussion. Topics can be: How the Tax Laws Affect You, Get Some Estate Planning Benefits *Now.* How to Provide for Retirement in Changing Economic Conditions, How to Leave More Money and Fewer Estate Difficulties for Your Heirs. Why Consider a Trust? Is Joint Tenancy Better Than a Will? Best to select something in the current news.

The speaker or panel. I have found good speakers among lawyers, trust officers, financial planners, etc. They must be experts, but be sure they can put themselves across. Look for a winning personality.

Prospect followup. As to followup, you might pass out something like the form shown in figure 4-1.

Fig. 4.1 *Sample prospect follow-up form.*

Please indicate areas of interest: ______________________

NAME ______________________________________

ADDRESS ___________________________________

CITY ______________________ ZIP ___________

PHONE _____________________________________

_________ Please call me to arrange a confidential interview to discuss my financial plans.

_________ Please send me information on how charitable giving can have tax and income benefits.

_________ Please include me on your invitation list for future sessions on financial planning.

The following might be interested in receiving mailings on gifts which pay income:

____

____

____

The following might be interested in an invitation to your next seminar or in a personal discussion: _____

____

____

THE VALUE OF YOUR REPUTATION

After giving talks for a while, you will become known as an authority. I always make clear that I am not a lawyer or C.P.A. at the beginning of the talk. In spite of that, I have been surprised and flattered to have lawyers and trust officers call me for advice on charitable trusts.

People will come to you with financial questions and this is often a golden opportunity to establish rapport with your prospective donors. You can supply information on taxes and other legal matters, but always be sure to include the magic phrase "consult your own attorney."

I help with the problem, even if it does not seem to relate to a gift. But I decline to prepare income tax returns or to take over financial management. I have, however, been glad to earn some consulting fees occasionally. But watch it. One friend got so busy making talks around the country and doing consulting that he got fired from his regular job. In fact, he finally ended up becoming a college president. So let that be a warning.

Your reputation as an authority and someone worth talking to will be most quickly earned through public appearances. Prepare for them well and the results will amaze you.

FINAL TIPS

Put your message in a story. Tell a human interest story. Describe your donor in enough detail to make her come to life; especially why she made the gift, what it accomplished and what it did for *her.*

Have a story for each type of gift you wish to present. Pack in emotional power.

Prepare thoroughly. You should know each story so well you need no notes.

Be part of the audience. Do not get behind a podium or have a written text. Stand directly in front of your audience, as close as you can get—so you can sense their participation.

If you wish to read a poem, a regulation citation or set of statistics, fine! Pull the paper out of your pocket, read it and return it to your pocket. Do not keep a paper or other barrier between you and your audience.

Chapter 5

USE DIRECT MAIL AS A MEANS, NOT AN END

"Let's send out a mailing." Board members are all too ready to say that when the subject of gift promotion comes up. Not a bad idea. A sound mailing program can bring results, even all by itself. Many bequests are created and outright gifts mailed because an effective letter arrived at the right time.

Another advantage to the mail approach is that it is an easy program to begin. Consultants and various commercial groups will supply you with letters, folders, and whatever you need.

You may purchase a complete package, mailing lists, writing skills, etc. I am amazed at the number of companies and services offered. For example, in *Fund Raising Management* magazine, the pages at the end show listings like this:

Creative Services—169 company names
Mailing Lists—71 names
Materials & Supplies—5 names
Production Services—90 names

The Philanthropy Tax Institute (see Appendix for addresses) has been my primary source for instruction in tax seminars, reference books, folders, and mailing materials on deferred giving. It is convenient to have folders available on each trust plan, reasons for making a will, etc. I have complete confidence that the data are both correct and understandable. I have also had good results from the firms of Pentera, Newkirk, and Sharpe (see Appendix). Your choice of resource companies will be a big factor in your success. This is where the National Society of Fund Raising Executives and other groups pay off for you. Your colleagues will help you find the best consultants and sources of material.

THE EFFECTIVE MAILING PROGRAM

Why is mail so important in seeking major gifts? It may be your principal source of inquiries. The beginning of a gift idea may often be traced to a letter.

I owe a happy work experience to a mailing effort. The reason the American Cancer Society, Missouri Division, hired me, to work part time after retirement, was that they had tried a quarterly deferred giving mailing with Newkirk. This resulted in a 3- to 4-percent return, but no one had the time and expertise to reply to the stack of inquiries. So they employed me to do something with those inquiry slips.

I was disappointed. Few were worthwhile. I eventually contacted every one, but it was 90 percent a waste of time. Why?

1. *The time factor.* An inquiry must be answered promptly. These were cold. Most had forgotten why they had sent in the reply slip.
2. *Poor list*. The names were obtained from local offices where the easiest thing to do was to put down names of prominent people in town and of American Cancer Society volunteers. Wonderful people! Dedicated to community service in a big way! But most did not have enough surplus money to consider a major gift.

My job was to ruthlessly weed out the list. This eliminated college presidents, hospital administrators, ministers, executive directors of other health organizations. Why were such people put in to start with? "I thought it would be nice to put him on the list, he is such a fine man." Sure, but he is a competitor, not a prospect.

I visited staff and volunteers all over the state to add prospects with money and with some reason to be interested in cancer. After that, an inquiry was more likely to mean something.

Check your list quality by phoning at random to discuss your last mailing. It will be worth your time to study mailing tests. By comparing your results over the years you will become very proficient.

Become an expert in the comparative effectiveness of various types of letters and folders.

Use human interest. Try to build a human interest story and facts about your organization into each folder. I did one called "A Gift That Pays You An Income for Life." This described a single lady, age seventy-two, who had only herself to depend on. It explained how her money was invested, her financial fears, and why she wanted to help her college. It gave specifics on how a gift annuity would increase her income and provide her the satisfaction of a major gift.

Use quotes, illustrations, photos, and captions in your folder to make your points quickly in an interesting way. I especially liked the mailings in which I wrote part of the copy and the rest was professionally prepared and dealt with tax news. This dual approach accomplished two things: a) it personalized the mailing in terms of the American Cancer Society; and b) it provided information of value to the reader.

Mailings to obtain bequests. Our best results were in bequest promotion. Bequests increased several hundred thousand dollars per year as a result of personal calls, seminars, and mailings. The latter reached more people and were the most important.

Your letter will be timed right—sometimes. Timing is all-important in getting a bequest provision. Your letter may happen to arrive just when your prospect:

1. Learns of the death of a dear friend from cancer.
2. Has just heard his own doctor caution him about cancer.
3. Comes into unexpected money.
4. Decides to revise his will before a long trip.
5. Faces his sixty-fifth birthday, etc.

Send enough letters to a good prospect and one will finally arrive at the right time, maybe just as he is about to see his lawyer about his will.

Watch your mailings to your publics. Have enough money to use the *right quality* for *your publics.* Don't invite such statements as "They must have a lot of money to mail anything this fancy," or, just as bad, "They must be on their last legs to put out anything this cheap."

I once wrote a human interest story about a doctor who established a deferred gift annuity, intending it for use in a small mailing and handout piece. I still like the story, but it was printed on cheap paper and crowded together too much. The appearance was uninviting and it was hard to read. My prospects were physicians who had an extra $5,000 or $10,000—so color, good paper, white space, and some headlines for quick comprehension would have been better. My fault was not to be sure it was done in the right way.

Your mailings gradually present all aspects of your case statement, why the prospect should give to you.

Be factual, direct, simple—above all, be absolutely honest. Your letters and brochures should build up confidence in you and in your organization.

If you sound like some commercial advertising, too much fluff, you will turn people off.

Convey honesty and integrity.

Avoid extreme statements.

Be conversational and pleasant. Maybe even admit a few shortcomings. Your mailings are part of the friend-making process.

Follow up, follow up, follow up. Yes, you can get a nice number of gifts by mail. Maybe even enough, if your needs are small. However, mailings are usually just one important part of a full program.

The inquiry you get from a mailing may be the beginning of a major gift. But, usually, it must be followed with phone calls for appointments, personal calls, help from volunteers, and proposals.

For more information on using direct mail fund raising, read *Dear Friend: Mastering the Art of Direct Mail Fund Raising,* by Kay Portney Lautman and Henry Goldstein (see Appendix A).

Chapter 6

BE SENSITIVE TO PROSPECTS' NEEDS

Older members of our society are often your best prospects for major gifts. They are usually well established in their careers, just retired, or in the sunset of their lives. Those of us past retirement age are well aware that we're not as young as we used to be. To varying degrees, the spring in our step is not quite as high, we're reluctant to change, we assimilate information more slowly. We're no less human, however, and deserve the dignity to which our years and contributions entitle us.

But we older folks are just part of your prospect pool. There are many different age groups, with varying concerns and radically different backgrounds. It is important in dealing with the various segments of your prospect list that you be sensitive to any special needs or concerns. Tailor your contact style to the prospect—always. Do this, and you will be able to effectively communicate your story, overcome objections, and land the major gift when others might not be successful.

WHEN THE PROPS ARE GONE

Indecision is often an obstacle. How do you deal with it? (I hope none of my friends of retirement age read this. They might resent it. If I could reply personally, I would say, "But you are the exception." There are many over age seventy or eighty who make decisions very well.)

Dealing with indecision. Let me tell you about someone who found this a problem and worked out a solution. My friend Will established trusts for retired Florida residents. He was kind enough to reveal to me his very effective selling procedures.

The prospect was usually a retired executive who had had big responsibilities. Why should he have so much difficulty now in making a decision? Visualize his present situation.

His decision-making props are gone—the big desk, dictating

machine, secretary, assistants, files, intercom. He was used to giving instructions to his secretary, calling in subordinates to hear his decisions, asking colleagues for opinions—but now all the decision-making apparatus has disappeared.

Present him with a proposal for a trust and he will take it home and put it on the coffee table. Soon it will be buried under magazines and newspapers, never to be read. My friend's procedure was as follows:

1. General meeting with prospects for presentation of personal trust plans. The ones I attended were crowded with prosperous, happy couples, recently retired to the land of sunshine.
2. Personal conference in the office. If prospects are married, be sure both are present.
3. Closing, or getting commitment, at the end of the conference.

During the office meeting, Will wrote all the facts in crayon on an easel (so there was nothing to take home), complete in every detail such as:

Funds to be put into the trust.
Trust management.
Possible withdrawals.
Yields.
How income paid.
Handling after death.

When all questions were answered, Will presented the trust agreement and described it in detail. Then he said, "Sign here."

Will told me, "Don't talk too fast. Be clear. Don't mumble. Speak with enough volume to be understood but don't shout, even if they are a little deaf. If you let them leave with only a promise to think it over, you have lost them."

That is tough and I never applied the method 100 percent, but I learned enough to be more forceful at times.

Go for the decision. You can be your usual charming self 99 percent of the time, but then you must finally ask for a decision. Your effort to close must be powerful. Carry the day against the tendency to indecision.

THE NONRESPONSIVE PROSPECT

After their initial enthusiasm, prospects will often seem to change their minds. They will raise "I can't give" objections at the last possible minute, causing you to wonder why you bothered in the first place. But you can get around some of these roadblocks when others can't if you borrow a technique or two from our marketing and sales colleagues, techniques I have used successfully. Some common objections and how to overcome them follow. Keep in mind, however, that people *do* change their mind. Your job is not to pressure, but rather to make sure the decision is based on a full understanding by the donor of the issues involved, and that you have covered all your bases in presenting the opportunity.

"I would like to make a large gift to the school, but have to consider retirement income for myself."

This is an opening to present the benefits to your prospect of a charitable remainder trust with lifetime income, a tax deduction now and an eventual big gift which is definite and can be publicly acknowledged.

I received an inquiry from a widow in a distant small town who said she wanted to give her home to the American Cancer Society if it would provide her more income. A friend had mentioned a letter I sent describing the gift of a home, retaining life occupancy. We discussed that and also how a unitrust could be funded with some of her certificates of deposit *and* her home. I gave her a proposal, she accepted it and made an appointment for us to see her lawyer. His response: "Put what you want in your will and don't bother with this complicated trust agreement." Afterward, she said to me and to her favorite niece when we returned to her home, "I will *not* make a will." I replied, "You have fourteen nieces and nephews who, without a will, must share equally in your estate after the settlement costs. The only one who has come to see you or helped you in any way is Mary here. She is a highly qualified accountant and has done so much for you in both business and in personal ways, but will receive the same as the thirteen you do not wish to give anything to." Her reply, "I will be dead so I will not care."

Did that mean she would do nothing for the American Cancer

Society and for Mary? No, the answer is to turn her selfishness into an advantage by having our lawyer prepare a trust which provides her with increased income, then give the trust instrument to her attorney for him to obtain her signature. The main problem to watch for is to make sure her attorney feels no embarrassment that he did not know about this particular type of trust. He will be reassured that the plan was approved by Dave Cornfeld, of St. Louis, an American Cancer Society volunteer and one of the best attorneys in the charitable remainder trust field.

"I hate to pay another attorney fee."

This is a signal to present a folder on wills and to offer the *free* services of a well qualified volunteer attorney for a preliminary discussion of estate plans. Only the preliminary discussion of various possibilities is free. The actual trust or will must be drawn by the donor's attorney.

"I am out of money."

Most numerous are the "cash-poor" objections.

I called on the president and owner of an engineering company who spent the first fifteen minutes in a detailed description of his son's college expenses. He ended with "Of course, with four years of this ahead, I cannot do anything for *your* college." Sounds reasonable, but I happened to know his personal income from his business and properties was over $1 million per year. So, was my call a failure?

No, it was just a rough beginning. I told a volunteer, who was in equal financial circumstances, about it and he said, "I'll talk to him and tell about my $25,000 gift to the college." That worked fine and produced another $25,000 gift from a prospect who had appeared to decline.

What good did my call do? It introduced the subject. Even though the prospect said "No," it was an automatic reaction to the approach of a fund raiser and not to be taken seriously. I did lay a groundwork of facts in preparation for the closing call by the volunteer. Incidentally, the volunteer got a big laugh out of the college expense recital and that helped give him the urge to nail his friend for trying to mislead me.

"I haven't gotten to it yet."

The "Procrastinators" are also with us in great numbers. When being briefed for my first trip west for The Menninger Foundation, I was told of a lady in San Francisco who kept saying she would give $10,000 but never did. "Forget her" was the advice of my experienced colleague who had talked with her three times. "She can't make up her mind."

I found the prospect to be elderly, living alone in a condo at the top of Nob Hill, in great need of some help in getting things done. For example, she wanted to sell property in Los Angeles, so I made all the arrangements for her and she was happy to get that settled. She found $20,000 in bearer bonds in her bureau drawer, so I saw that they got to her bank: $10,000 into her trust fund and $10,000 for The Menninger Foundation Pooled Fund. She was no longer able to entirely care for herself and wanted to move into a retirement home, but thought she could not sell her top-floor condo. She did not realize the market value of her tremendous view of the Golden Gate Bridge and the Bay. I found a very capable young lady to handle the sale who had sold several condos in the same building. The proceeds go to a charitable remainder trust paying her income for life. I verified the desirability of the retirement home she was considering and saw that she completed and turned in her application. The Nob Hill condo will eventually bring The Menninger Foundation much more than the $10,000 which was our first objective. But it took several calls to find the reasons for procrastination and to determine how to get things moving. Cultivation often means helping the prospect remove a variety of obstacles to the action you seek.

I had a prospect in Palo Alto who wished to make a large gift and was well able to do so. But all she wanted to talk about were the problems her daughter was having in the San Francisco area with divorce, new job, moving, etc. etc. My prospect asked me to go to see her daughter and to find out the true situation. I called on the daughter twice and discovered she was handling her problems very well. The mother was reassured and we could then talk about the gift.

Another time I presented a trust plan to an older single lady and thought we had covered everything in our three visits. Not only did she live in a distant state, but her home was a long drive by rental car over the mountains from the airport. I was concerned that she seemed reluctant to sign. Would I have to make another trip? She finally said, "I didn't tell you yet about my cousin. She was left with three young children to support and is having a terrible time to make ends meet. I want to do something for her." Fine, it was a simple change to make. The original agreement provided income to donor for life, then to her brother. The brother was near death and rich. We substituted the cousin's name for her brother and the agreement was finished. There is a reason for procrastination. Dig for it.

"I can't possibly burden you with this property—it's losing money!"

This opens the way for a survey and proposal on a unitrust which pays only income earned, up to the percentage chosen with make-up—a feasible way for your institution to hold property until the right time to sell.

Some of you may wonder how to fund a unitrust with real estate or securities which pay little or nothing but have growth potential if held for a few years. Let's say the trust corpus is appraised at $200,000, the net income is $1,000 per year, and the trust is obligated to pay 8 percent or $16,000 per year to the donor. Specify "make-up" in the trust instrument. Then there is no obligation by the trustee to pay more than the net earnings. But later the property is sold for $400,000 and invested at 10 percent. The entire $40,000 per year income will be paid to the donor until the deficiency of previous years is made up. After that, the income will be 8 percent times the principal as valued each year.

"But there will be an estate tax. I hate paying taxes!"

Many wealthy people hate to pay taxes. Make sure the donor understands from you or from the legal advisor how a charitable trust can reduce or avoid the tax burden on the final estate of the surviving spouse.

WHEN ALL IS NOT WHAT IT SEEMS

The most exasperating case of misleading by a prospect happened soon after I started working part time for the American Cancer Society in Missouri. My job was to start a new program in deferred giving, an addition to the already burdened budget (some said more promotion expense was not needed). I was eager to make a good impression—to demonstrate the value of my years of experience. That was when a prospect made a fool of me.

On November 27, 1979, our unit director phoned me with this exciting news: "A little old lady wants to give her home to the American Cancer Society."

I found that the prospect was suffering from terminal cancer and that her husband had died of cancer a year before. She showed me her attractive, well-built, saleable home and also where she was moving to be close to relatives. Mrs. N. stated that title was held jointly with her late husband who was a builder and had built this home. We set a time for her to turn over the deed and execute transfer to the American Cancer Society.

On the day of transfer I went to the abstract company and found that she had already given a half interest to her niece. She denied having done that and wanted me to get the half interest back for her so she could give the entire property to the American Cancer Society.

After wasting time and mileage on more complications, I decided there was no intention of making a gift, just a clumsy effort by relatives to use the Society for their own purposes—mostly to get revenge on the niece holding the half interest.

You will get an inquiry like this once every few years. It may look OK (as this did) but turn out to be a waste of time. All you can do is check it out. But most prospects are sincere.

Once you win the full confidence and friendship of the prospect, you can count on hearing the truth. Allow time and a few visits to reach that point, then provide your donor with the thrill of creating a big gift.

SENTIMENT AS MOTIVATION

Sentiment and nostalgia become increasingly important to the elderly.

On behalf of Baker University I visited a lady in a small Kansas town, after a briefing by her pastor. He sent me on my way with these words, "Yes, it will be nice for you to visit her. She will appreciate a call from an administrator of her college." Maybe he thought I was employed just to make goodwill calls.

In the course of our conversation, I described an important and urgent project at the college, which would have appealed to her late husband. I stressed his devotion to the college and she had tears in her eyes as she told stories of how much Baker meant to him. I then asked her for $10,000 for the project which involved so much sentimental value. She wrote a check for that amount without another word, thinking what a wonderful memorial to her husband.

An amusing sidelight. Before leaving town I phoned the minister to tell him the good results of the call. He was amazed. Probably no one in this town had ever made such a large gift (or even thought of it). Then he became angry and said to all who would listen, "That guy came down here and took $10,000 out of my church." If the minister, or a member of his board, had asked her in an appealing way for something important—she would have given him $10,000 anytime since she loved her church. But that minister had no idea of ever trying to get such a big gift. She had made it clear to me that she had lots of money and wanted to help her church even more than her college. Sorry, they wouldn't let sentiment work for the church as it did for our college.

A LITTLE EXTRA ATTENTION

Older people respond especially well to personal attention. Some are lonely. Many do not feel appreciated.

I have a pooled income fund with The Menninger Foundation and receive a quarterly dividend check. The other pooled funds I have are handled in a routine way and attempt nothing to build goodwill. But when Phil Menninger handled those checks, he always sent me a personal letter which mentioned his vacation in Maine, a bicycle trip or a change at The Foundation. Maybe that special attention is partly why I have added to that fund and not to the others.

When Betty and I visited the beautiful new West Campus recently, Phil happened to see us and dropped everything to be the genial host.

President Dr. Roy Menninger writes occasionally wtih news of The Foundation to help us continue to feel part of this great medical achievement.

Extra time and thoughtfulness for your older prospects will

be well worth the effort. You may even consider it your most productive work time. Note, for example, the cheery birthday greeting from Phil Menninger in fig. 6-1.

Fig. 6.1

June 16

Happy
Birthday!

Phil

One of Phil's short notes on routine check transmittals is shown in fig. 6-2; note the personal touch still included.

Fig. 6.2

July 18, 1979

Mr. and Mrs. Charles F. Mai
20 Springer Drive
Columbia, Missouri 65201

Dear Betty and Charlie:

Enclosed is your quarterly payment on the Pooled Income Fund.

When you get this, the family and I will be enjoying a brief vacation in Maine. Hope your summer is pleasant.

Sincerely,

Phil

Philip B. Menninger
Director, Planned Giving

PBM:mf

Chapter 7

SEEK THE DEFERRED GIFT

One reason I enjoy deferred and major giving so much is that there are two quite different sides to the job.

It is fun to meet people, make friends, see new places, speak to audiences—get out from behind the desk to be with the people who will provide the funds for our organization to do a first-rate job. That is exciting.

I also appreciate some days, or at least hours, of peace and quiet in my office. A time to study investments, economic developments, tax changes, and the situation of a particular prospect. This is an opportunity to be creative, to make research and analysis pay off for the donor.

I couldn't sit at a desk all the time and I couldn't pound the sidewalks every day, all day. But I love the combination. Does it appeal to you?

YOU CAN LEARN DEFERRED GIVING

Many development people avoid deferred giving because they think there is too much to learn. Not so. The specialized legal knowledge you need is available from lawyers. In fact, you will need a lot of professional help in a variety of fields. You can learn the pros and cons of various trusts in a few hours and that is primarily what you need.

Nice to be an expert. If you work in trusts and estates long enough, go to schools and study tax publications—you may become something of an expert. Prospects will come to you for advice. Fine! But you don't have to start that way.

The problem simplified. Your objective is to present to the donor the advantages of a major gift, inspire the excitement of participating in an important program. If part of the gift needs to be deferred, just include it in the package. The tax and legal aspects are of minor importance, but must be covered.

For example, your prospect says your facilities for teaching business are inadequate. He says you need a computer lab, a beautiful lecture hall for distinguished visiting speakers (such as himself), etc.

He will give $2 million outright for construction, plus $500,000 for future expansion and $500,000 for improvements and maintenance. He wants a modest lifetime income for himself on the second two gifts. Depending on actual costs during construction and how much you get in other gifts, he may add to all three funds next year.

All you need to say is, "Yes, we can do it. With the help of our attorney and architect, I will prepare a proposal for you."

WHY DEFERRED GIFTS ARE IMPORTANT

Your institution will be able to plan better with the assurance of funds to come. At the same time, donors reap a variety of benefits from deferred giving. Deferred gifts:

—Memorialize the donor's life. People want to be remembered, see their names on plaques and honor rolls.
—Provide self-fulfillment. Givers desire a significant role in a worthwhile project.
—Can be honored and recognized at board meetings, special dinners, etc.
—Protect income for those named as lifetime beneficiaries.
—Confer tax advantages.
—Make larger gifts possible, as compared to cash gifts.
—Relinquish investment burdens.
—Are less vulnerable to attack by disgruntled heirs.
—Facilitate control of property after death by trust provisions.
—Provide privacy and avoid publicity involved in will probate.
—Constitute the best way to make a substantial gift with little or no reduction in income.

HOW TO OBTAIN INFORMATION

I changed from general fund raising with responsibilities in administration, public relations, student recruiting, and special events to work as a deferred giving specialist. I liked it because I could concentrate on one prospect at a time. This meant I could do a lot of research in the preparation of each proposal. I was at various times and places Development Director, Assistant to the President, Vice President, and Acting President. That experience helped in talking to prospects about their special program interests. I learned a lot from tax schools, development seminars, and reading, but putting a lot of time into each case is how I learned the work. I eventually felt comfortable speaking to bar association groups, C.P.A.s, estate planners, insurance meetings, etc. The fact that I had no law degree did not bother me in dealing with lawyers, because I was well informed from tax letters and reference books and had more practical experience in this one specialized area of charitable gifts than most of the attorneys I dealt with. For resources on deferred giving, see Appendix B.

WHEN TO SPECIALIZE

I enjoy deferred giving work. It is satisfying to have plenty of time to do a good job with each prospect. I appreciate very much that my employers were willing to spend the money for me to get the expensive training which made me an expert in this type of promotion. I had as a youth wanted to be a lawyer, doctor, professor, or something professional. Now I am a professional. I can tell that by the number of people who ask for free advice.

Incidentally, many of my efforts to be helpful without charge have been useless. Does a doctor prescribe without an examination? I suggest this answer, "You have an interesting fund-raising problem which requires fact gathering, analysis, and evaluation by a professional. Your best move is to employ a consultant."

If you are a top administrator in a nonprofit organization who is tired of too many meetings, endless reports, and the procession of people coming into your office—consider deferred giving. Especially if you enjoy helping people achieve their giving objectives and if some travel is attractive. However, you can be anybody with a gift for friendship and who will study tax and financial matters relating to each case.

Some say that most prospects are retired or at least over 55 years of age and used to dealing with male attorneys and other advisors, so a deferred giving specialist should be an older man, 55 years of age or more. Don't believe it! Middle-age and younger women can be the best. The main qualities for this job are not much related to age or sex.

TIPS FOR THE DEFERRED GIFT SPECIALIST

You are likely to be your own boss, because no one else knows how to do it. They trust you, hope for the best and believe your wonderful expectancy reports. Very nice. This solid backing from your management does wonders for your self-confidence.

Beware of any lawyer on the board who sees no need to keep up to date on IRS regulations, U.S. Tax Court Decisions, and revisions of the Code as they affect charitable gifts. That may not stop him from laying down rules for you, often *through* your president. How do you tell an honored and experienced lawyer, "Check the law," especially if he controls or influences one or more big trusts?

Qualify the prospect. Another warning: don't become too fascinated by the marvels you can achieve with charitable trusts. Occasionally, you will get a specific inquiry about such a trust. The tendency is to joyfully delve into the financial and legal aspects, forgetting to check out the most important element in a cultivation: motivation.

I was delighted to receive an inquiry about trusts from a lady in St. Louis in response to our quarterly tax letter mailing. When I phoned for an appointment, she said, "Maybe I would like to talk about a trust if I could get a lifetime income." She set a time and said it must be when her husband was not home because she did not want him to know what she intended. When I arrived, the house was in the process of complete redecoration and all new furniture was purchased. Reason: she did not want to be reminded of the previous wife. She immediately began describing her extensive holdings inherited from her first husband, why her current husband did not need her money, the importance of providing for her son, age sixteen, and what to do if her son marries and that she needed a better plan for her investments. A wonderful opportunity to put my knowledge of trusts to work! I devised three trusts to accomplish everything she wanted, the largest of which was a charitable remainder trust with the American Cancer Society as ultimate beneficiary. She said, "Why should I do anything for the American Cancer Society?" I began to realize that my own interest in a chance to show what can be done with trusts led me to do a lot of work which resulted in nothing. This lady soon became preoccupied with getting a divorce and did nothing about creating my beautifully constructed trusts. I did not qualify this prospect to start with. Don't lose sight of fund raising basics, no matter how expert you become in estate planning.

Use your volunteer pool. Be sure you have plenty of volunteer help to identify prospects, arrange appointments, make cultivation calls, help prepare proposals, and serve as resource people in technical areas. Board members and large donors will help you. Set up a Deferred Giving Council and keep it busy. Arrange prospect evaluation meetings. You may have specialized committees in life insurance, brokers, investment counselors, trust officers, attorneys, C.P.A.s, etc. They will help you with estate planning seminars, work as a group to solve a tough problem, etc.

There is a tendency for your president and board to prefer outright gifts because money is needed *NOW.* This preference may be reciprocated by the donor who finds it easier to sign a small check than to have a lawyer draw up a complicated agreement or write a codicil. The answer is to prepare a statement, selections from which you will present over and over as appropriate. Keep reminding management why deferred gifts are important.

Interview objectives. Don't expect to answer every possible question on the first interview. Leave the door open to phone or return for more data.

These are your objectives:

1. Motivation for a major gift to your organization.
   —Approach this from the emotional side, "Tell me about your feelings for our hospital."
   —Take plenty of time on this one.
   —Until you have established a powerful desire to give, why go ahead?
   —Go even to the point of discovering the particular project which sparks the most interest, perhaps a new machine to help save lives.
2. Assets and liabilities.
   —I have been stopped at this point. Unless the donor has ample resources for his/her own and family needs, do not try to get him/her interested in a big gift.
   —If you consider a charitable trust funded by property, get all the details such as location, market value, mortgages, how title held, condition, rentals, offers made, etc. Avoid property not readily saleable.
   —Pay special attention to appreciated stocks, bonds, or real estate which pay little or no net income. Perhaps you can show how the donor may receive *increased* income plus a charitable deduction with your charitable trust.
   —Compare net assets, present income, and living ex-

penses. Then you can develop an idea for size and type of charitable gift.

3. Objects of bounty: relatives, friends, charities.
   —Your plan should provide for *everyone*. If you miss a person or a cause in your plan, that omission may cause a decision to be put off.

Usually, it is best to be conversational in manner, appear relaxed. When the prospect is talking along the lines you want to know about, give encouragement briefly with a nod, smile, or unobtrusive comment. Say, "That's interesting" or, "Tell me more about that" or, "Keep going about your cousin and how you would help her" or, "It sounds like you wish to benefit your friend who has helped you so much" or "Are you saying you really want to leave out your half-sister?"

Watch body language, notice what sparks the most interest. Observe withdrawal motions.

Take notes and have plenty of paper. Review your notes with the prospect and be glad you left room in your notes for the additions and changes which will be made in the review. Your donor wants you to get everything exactly right and *in writing*.

What you learn is confidential, even if nothing is said about that.

While your primary concentration during the interview will be listening, you may find opportunities to establish yourself as a source of information on financial matters such as taxes as related to charities. For example, you might describe how the Tax Reform Act of 1986 made few changes in the rules governing charitable trusts. Or you might explain the previous rules, prior to December 31, 1986, on preferential treatment for long-term capital gains—as compared to the present treatment of all capital gains as ordinary income.

Subscribe to a good taxletter such as "Taxwise Giving" (see Appendix for the address of The Philanthropy Tax Institute). This will provide you with items about how taxes affect families and estate planning. Quote a section of the Code, a recent U.S. Tax Court decision, a proposed IRS Regulation to keep your people fully informed.

One purpose of the Tax Reform Act of 1986 was to reduce the need to think taxes in any business transaction—but tax liability must still be considered—and you should be one to help with this.

Chapter 8

DON'T BE AFRAID OF REAL ESTATE

In the midst of computers opening new horizons and tremendous fund-raising efforts at every turn—here is an overlooked area waiting for you to seize the opportunity—search out big real estate gifts.

Doesn't the idea of big money in real estate gifts sound exciting? It seems logical that real estate brokers would embrace this opportunity to benefit your charity while possibly earning commissions themselves.

If you could visualize all the possible gifts you might obtain in the next few years, some of the largest would be in real estate. But those might require the most in imagination and in hard work from you and from your volunteers. There are ways to lighten your work load.

SPOTTING THE GOOD DEAL

With a competent real estate broker, study your area for property which might be ready for giving to you. Don't look for the finest and newest. Find property not so attractive, but saleable.

Think saleable, rather than attractive. In an area of beautiful new apartment and condo buildings, each with the latest in health club equipment, there may be nearby some old garden apartments. Look to see if they are no longer properly maintained because they are losing out to competition. Check the records for who owns one. It may be someone in his seventies or eighties in declining health, tired of hearing about plumbing breaks, peeling paint, vandalism, a crack in the swimming pool and so forth. He would like to sell, but does not want to pay tax on the profit. He supposes he should convert to condominiums, but that is a big undertaking. You have a message he is ready to hear. Trade a headache for an income tax deduction which will pay for the finest Caribbean cruise he can imagine. Or maybe he is not in a high tax bracket and needs more income. Perhaps this owner gets no net return at all, after taxes and constantly increasing maintenance. If the property will sell for $200,000, the trust might pay him 8 percent for life; $16,000 per year with no worries is better than distressing phone calls late at night with no net income from the property.

You and your real estate friends may find an old hotel no longer profitable, but in a valuable location.

Locate a vacant service station, target of vandalism. Maybe the owner will be glad to be rid of such an eyesore and worry.

There are old office buildings in areas no longer fashionable for offices but saleable for other purposes. Their broken windows could mean dollars for you.

Rental houses become worse problems with age, but may be on saleable land.

Don't be greedy. If you decide to offer a charitable remainder trust, don't be too greedy. Other charities may be more important to your potential donor. Better to recognize that and take 20 percent than get nothing. The National Benevolent Association was once reported to not accept a trust unless they received at least 50 percent of the remainder. Why? Wouldn't you take even 10 percent if the principal amount were $1 million? I would rather have $100,000 than see it all go elsewhere.

How to spot the con artist. There are some cautions. I always wanted to meet a confidence man, prince of crooks—but never expected to find one offering a gift to a charity. This one contacted the president of my college who then reached me in Boston late on a Friday afternoon as I was about to relax and head for a plane home after a full week of calls. My boss said, "Be in California tomorrow morning to receive a gift of a patent." The gentleman was fairly convincing until he asked for good faith money up front. I knew it was a con and confirmed this with the attorney general of California. The latter told me of another con artist who gave land to a local college which turned out to be mortgaged by fraudulent representations for far more than its value. This trickster was giving away a debt and getting a charitable deduction by means of a false appraisal.

Too good to be true. Sometimes you may have to turn down what appears, at first, to be a wonderful gift.

I was told that a doctor in southern Illinois wanted to give property to the American Cancer Society. When I went to see him I found it was a novitiate consisting of dormitories, chapel, swimming pool, workshop, dining room, classrooms, and a home on about fifteen acres. The doctor thought it would be useful to us as a retreat, but it was too far from Chicago. He estimated the replacement value at over $1 million, and I thought that very conservative. The reason he and his wife owned it was curious. His wife inherited property in Eastern Europe which had been used for training priests. The only way to transfer anything to the United States was to exchange for similar property here (if you do not understand that, neither do I). The doctor's purpose was simply to turn this property into a charitable deduction against his substantial income as owner of a clinic.

A local banker, a real estate agent, and others active in the Society made a determined effort and found there was no market to sell this property. A special committee of the board decided not to accept the offer. Rather a thrill to decline a $1 million gift!

The doctor finally got the local school board to accept everything for school purposes. He was lucky.

When to avoid some property gifts. A woman was interested in giving sixteen houses in Kansas City slum property, but it was too difficult to sell and to maintain while trying to find a buyer. We dropped it.

We were offered a vacant warehouse in Chicago. Since it had been for sale so long, we turned it down. When I passed it frequently on the freeway and continued to see the "For Sale" sign and broken glass everywhere, I felt the decision was right.

Don't refuse the small gift. Don't overlook the small gifts. The Illinois Division of the American Cancer Society had a number of very small oil leases which seemed to involve almost as much accounting expense as the total amount of royalties. A friend in the trust department of the First National Bank in Chicago told me of a man whose business it was to buy such items, and we easily converted them all into cash for fighting cancer.

SEEK THE RIGHT EXPERT HELP

When we were offered underground coal rights in Illinois, I had to visit and inquire in a nearby town for a coal lawyer to handle this transaction involving the future value of rights. As in so many other real estate deals, I was lost without expert help (usually given gladly and at no charge).

You need to locate a competent professional who is dedicated to your cause. That is important. Then you must keep after him, go with him to examine properties, look up ownership records at the courthouse and listen to the owners. This is a lot of work and took more time than I could find as a part-timer. How can you do better?

You might find a retired real estate broker who will volunteer a lot of his time to search the city and examine records for you. He can get the facts on what will sell, may know some of the owners and how to approach them.

For a property you are interested in, ask your broker volunteer for a market analysis or competitive market analysis. Learn and use his terminology.

In short, don't be afraid to get your feet wet. Treading where others fear to can pay off for you in the years ahead.

Chapter 9

DEVELOP THYSELF, DEVELOPMENT DIRECTOR

This chapter is directed to those fund raisers who have the formal responsibility for managing a fund-raising program. Whether you have the title of development director or not, as a manager you have a unique opportunity to improve your chances of getting that major gift. The wisdom of the axiom, "Physician, heal thyself" applies to the fund raiser as well. Don't overlook the gains to be made by continued education and self-improvement. None of us are ever perfect, and if my experience is any indication, there is always more to learn.

MANAGE YOUR TIME FOR RESULTS

Two objectives sometimes tend to collide with each other; they are

1. To use each minute constructively
2. To answer every inquiry as completely as you can. Don't miss a lead to a big gift.

But some inquiries are no good. I have agonized over how time can be wasted. I will give you an example and defy you to tell me how I could have handled this better.

My boss sent me a letter with this note attached: "Charlie, please check this out."

The letter offered the Society a house in a small town near the Ozark resort areas to use in a lottery.

I knew we were not interested in the lottery idea and verified that. My boss had no more information. I discovered from volunteers in his town that the writer was a real estate man of good repute.

From the letter it might be inferred that he wanted to give us the house. If saleable, that was O.K. We could sell and use the proceeds for the cause.

The worst feature of this situation was that I was going through this man's town the next week. Easy to check it out, so it seemed.

I was unable to qualify him on the phone, but made an appointment. I was fifteen minutes early and he was fifteen minutes late. During that half hour of conversation with the others in his office, I decided he was not a prospect and was leaving when the prospect walked in. I wanted to ask two or three questions and dispose of the matter quickly, but he insisted we visit the house, which turned out to be his own home.

The deal was he wanted to *sell* us the house at full market price and he offered no gift of house, money, or time. He admitted that he had no charitable intention. I tried to be reasonably nice but made it clear the Society had no interest in buying his house.

The purpose of telling this is to demonstrate how some waste of time is part of the job. Sure, try to qualify by phone, ask volunteers for background, check your records, etc. But accept the fact that inquiries must be answered and that a few will only result in loss of valuable time.

That is one reason I like to handle the first response to an inquiry myself to make sure that a volunteer will not have a bad experience.

LEARN WHEN TO SELL HARD—AND SOFT

Is it best to be pleasant and indirect or to go directly to the point and push hard?

The answer, of course, depends on the prospect and the situation. If you make a survey, chances are you'll find that prospects prefer that you choose the easy, friendly way.

David McCord was excellent with this approach. His publishers called him "poet, essayist, and fund-raiser unique."

McCord described his style of fund raising at Harvard as "fishing with a barbless hook." He finally retired and with him went his tentative reminders launched against the "silence of the silent" for the Harvard Fund.

His alma mater switched fund-raising gears and drove home hard facts and strong appeals. That produced more results in money than the soft approach, much to the delight of the governing powers. McCord's gentle touch had been beautiful, but not enough to produce the desired result.

For you see, although a nostalgic view of Sever Hall may generate a feeling of warmth in the old grad, it is not likely to motivate him (or her) to reach for his checkbook. For a serious gift, the prospect had to at least be shown a well-prepared case statement, followed by a definite request.

When I started in college development, I spent many evenings looking at old photos, remembering professors, describing classmates, etc. It was a warm, happy time for the alumni, but no one thought to say, "Here's my gift to the alumni fund."

Nostalgia can be a factor in obtaining major gfts, but don't count on that alone.

Hard facts, but soft communication. Please do not think I am just advocating the hard sell. I believe that friendliness and understanding are always of supreme importance. However, in a very courteous way you must arrive at the point where you can say, "On behalf of the committee I am here to ask you for a $25,000 naming gift for a teacher's office in this new building we have been discussing. The committee wants to put a brass plaque on the door, 'In memory of Joseph Smith.' Is that the way you want the wording?" Usually it is better to have some such specific request ready to present in a clear and definite way.

Always in good taste. When McCord looked at his colleagues in other colleges, he feared that "our song has become pretty shrill and insistent." He warned against "pressure and repetition, parrot gab and gimmick language." He said this is in sharp contrast to the imagination and "contagious delight" we hope to find in our teachers. The selling of the product should reflect the good quality of the product itself. Better to put the appeal in human interest terms, even with humor, if you can manage that.

MASTER THE ART OF DOING LUNCH

If you are trying for a $100,000 gift and if your prospect is worth several million—what does it matter who pays?

In a recent NSFRE (National Society of Fund Raising Executives) meeting I discovered that this question bothers a lot of people so it has some importance. My answer: You extend the first invitation to lunch, dinner or tea and you pay. The second time (if you do o.k. the first time), you will be invited to the private club, home, or favorite restaurant. You may not be expected to pay any other time than the first.

But a few donors regard the free lunch as part of the deal. I was very fond of Mrs. Russell Stover and still buy Stover candy. She started making candy for sale in her own kitchen and became successful and wealthy, an excellent businesswoman and good company. Her swimming pool was the exact salt content of the ocean. It was fun to take our college students there for a swim and a surprise. They discovered why a shower stood beside the pool.

Mrs. Stover gave to sixty-five charities and they formed the center of her social life. I took her to her favorite restaurant, Putch's 210, once every six months and invited her to all events at the college. She was a generous donor but never paid for a lunch. Another development director told me how she operated and I was grateful to know how to keep her as a friend of the college.

USE, DON'T ABUSE, THE TELEPHONE

The telephone is a marvelous way to build friendship and to tell human interest stories. Some prospects like a casual approach, "It's a quiet day at the office and I got to thinking about the good talk we had about this time last month." Or, "Could we visit on the phone? How does your son like his new job?" Another prospect might prefer something definite and businesslike, "Did you see the article in today's *Wall Street Journal* on problems with certain municipal bonds? It reminded me of what you said last month."

QUALIFY YOUR PROSPECTS THROUGH MOTIVATION

It may be better to forget hard sell or soft sell. That is a superficial approach. You must go deeper to try for a major gift. Before asking for that $100,000 you must deal effectively with the most important factor in your success: motivation. Concentrate on finding and encouraging motivation. That will generate action.

Irvin G. Wyllie wrote in "Campus America" (See Appendix), "It is a rare report of alumni giving that illuminates the lives of donors" or reveals their *motives*. Wyllie believed that motivation can be better understood in considering historical figures.

History reveals motivation. Peter Cooper was a poor apprentice in New York who could find no training schools for the working classes. He felt this lack of formal education prevented him from raising his inventive genius to the highest potential. This provided a powerful motive to establish the Cooper Union so other young people would find ways to develop their talents.

Stephen Girard provided for orphans because of his own experience without father or mother.

Andrew Carnegie found great difficulty borrowing books as a boy living in a working class area. He felt libraries should be open to all who wanted to learn and to advance themselves.

Why did George Eastman give millions to establish dental clinics in Rochester and in many other cities? As a boy he endured the ordeal of watching an incompetent dentist yank fourteen teeth from his mother's mouth. Eastman found further motivation in his gifts to the University of Rochester: the cultural and social advantages of the University made life better for his employees and helped to attract highly skilled workers. He also felt an obligation to the city which helped him to be so successful.

Cornelius Vanderbilt was largely immune to charitable appeals made directly to him. But his second wife, Frank, could accomplish wonders such as the million dollars given to Vanderbilt University. Motivation could only be generated through his wife and through personal friendships she made possible.

Probe early for motivation. It is a bad mistake to forget about motivation. I received an inquiry about charitable trusts from Chesterfield, an expensive suburb west of St. Louis. After arranging an appointment, I was impressed on arrival at the prospect's home. It was artistically designed, with a huge tree growing out of a garden in the center and stood in beautiful grounds on the edge of a private lake.

She was a divorcée with no children, large means and was most anxious to learn more about investments, trusts, and everything related to her personal finances. Her advisor had performed poorly. She had more losers than winners and I thought he had not positioned her to benefit from future economic developments. I suggested certain courses, books, and publications for her own education. I was delighted to find a prospect so interested and ready to talk.

We spent three hours going over her portfolio, selecting stocks to put into a charitable trust and making sure there were no family obligations to consider. Then I asked, "Is the American

Cancer Society to be the sole charitable beneficiary after your death?" She replied, "I don't know, I guess so." Such enthusiasm! This lack of interest in the charitable gift disturbed me, so I went deeper, "Why are you interested in making a gift to the American Cancer Society?" She said, "Because my sister-in-law worked there a while and she told me about you. I am not involved with any charities and had not thought of any kind of gift."

No motivation. I should have found out sooner.

It took me over three hours to discover that the reason for her inquiry had nothing to do with the American Cancer Society. She just wanted to learn more about her financial holdings and to understand what she should do.

In summary. Go for motivation. Build your cultivation, your proposal and your close on that. Your style, whether easy or businesslike, gentle touch or hard sell, is not nearly as important as to find and work with your prospect's deep motivation. Your prospect will sell himself.

DEVELOP YOUR LEADERSHIP SKILLS

Outstanding leaders are a big factor in your success. What are the characteristics of a true leader?

The personal touch. Visits to customers—patients, students, donors, members—never run less than 30 percent of work time for senior line management and not less than 10 percent for indirect. Are your top people out in the field that much? Maybe, if meetings are counted. Perhaps we rely too much on large formal gatherings. All employees should have some contact with those being served.

Focus more on patients if working with a hospital, on students if working with a school, on potential or actual victims if working with a health organization, on members if working with a church.

Service. Hospital administrators should study Fredonia Jacques' *Verdict Pending: A Patient Representative's Intervention* (Cap istrano Press, 1983). The implications of "minor" slights are amazing.

I discovered the far-reaching results of patient treatment when I did some work for Saint Marys Hospital of the Mayo Clinic complex. One attorney in a small Minnesota town told a graphic story of how his daughter had been treated by various doctors only to get dramatically worse and was at the point of death when wheeled into the Mayo Clinic. It was estimated that she had fifteen minutes to live on arrival in the lobby. Immediate action saved her. Now she is back in college, active in tennis, and enjoying life as never before. Not only was this father pleased to have a visitor from the hospital who appreciated this story, complete with photos and many details, but he was receptive to the idea of a trust gift. Visualize the result if those crucial fifteen minutes had been spent waiting and answering questions in the admissions office.

How do you treat your "customers?" If you work in a hospital, have you gone through the admissions procedure yourself? In some hospitals it is an unpleasant ordeal at a time of acute stress. I have asthma and am very sensitive to tobacco smoke. After a severe attack, my doctor sent me to the hospital. I needed help right away. When the questions were finally over, the clerk mentioned I would have a roommate. I asked, "Are you sure he doesn't smoke?" She replied, "Yes, he smokes cigars." That meant more delay to find another room. That admissions clerk made me feel that she did not care about me or her job.

Does anyone listen to your patients complain about the hospital gown? Is the convenience of the medical people the only factor to consider? Look at what has been done to improve children's sections. Use similar imagination for adults who are possible future donors.

Beyond the call of duty. Excellent leaders make sure that receptionists, telephone operators, and all who contact the public are well trained in courtesy and in how to *go overboard* in being helpful. A wealthy alumna of a famous women's college, who gives several hundred thousand each year to various universities, told me an incredible story. In response to suggestions from me, she finally returned to visit her alma mater, but saw only the receptionist. This formidable lady on the desk in the administration building gave her the cold stare, did not offer a campus tour, provided no information, did not suggest she see anyone or that she visit any part of the campus. As the widow of a famous millionaire she was accustomed to more courtesy and was so offended that she dashed to her car and never returned to her own school. She gave her money to universities near her home where she was made welcome. When I told this story to college officials, it was greeted with a shrug and "That's how she is." Not good enough. They thought that a long-time, sour, underpaid, receptionist was not important compared to their other concerns. I felt like saying, "Look how many potential supporters that receptionist has lost for you."

John D. MacArthur made one of the great fortunes of this century and knew the importance of personal contact. At his Bankers Life & Casualty Co., he hired handicapped and retired people from the neighborhood to respond to customer calls and to letters by *individual* replies. They provided friendly and easy-to-understand answers.

Response to complaints. Complaints are a golden opportunity. The customer is aroused and ready to pay attention at the moment of the complaint. He expects the worst and any courtesy will go a long way. Make the response fast, highly personalized and include top management. Let the president phone on some complaints. Smother the complainer with kindness and you will make a friend.

Use staff and donors. Great management arranges for top staff and volunteers to get feedback by phone on, "How are we doing?" It might go like this. "Thank you for your gift of $10,000. Are you satisfied with how we are using your money? Do you have any suggestions for us?" Some negative stuff is also worth getting, wonderful for generating improvements. Select some who declined to give this year and ask for comments on the organization. Invite them to a special function. Have a gathering of large potential donors to *tell you* how to sell, who the big prospects are, and so forth. Ask, "How can we do better?"

Acknowledge contributions. Awards are important to dynamic leadership and must be staged for maximum impact. A TV executive went to a lot of work to prepare a clever, visual way of presenting an award. It took seven minutes. As my friend was getting up to begin, the chairman announced that no award would be allowed to take over one minute and that he was going to call time. Disaster.

Advance preparation allows leadership to shine through with great power in the giving of awards. Your very best leaders make the presentations and do so with enthusiasm and pleasure. They mean it. (And they know how much time is available.)

Involve your staff—and yourself. Do you get your employees together frequently, all of them, to make them feel part of the operation—more involved?

Charts, financial controls, surveys, time studies, computer analyses, even some dull meetings may all have a necessary place in management. But the new thinking is to concentrate on the human factors—face to face.

When I became a manager, I wanted to sit behind my big desk and tell people what to do, to enjoy the comfort of my impressive office and dictate memos. Wrong attitude! Terrible! The boss should spend at least two or three days per month out on the firing line with the troops. He should be the one to substitute when they are short of help in shipping, stock room, clerical, or whatever. The boss will become a better manager if he spends a day filling out those forms he approved and discovers how much useless information he required.

I noticed the manager making hamburgers in Wendy's. He was diligent and efficient. "You have two of your girls over there eating the lunch you just prepared for them. Why not have one of them help if you are short?" He replied, "This is their lunch break and then they make salads. I will have a substitute cook in soon." Respect for his people. Able and willing to do every job himself. Such qualities make that young man a manager. His employees listen to him. He has a great future.

I hope you are already an excellent manager. Fine! That may be the most important factor in your success as a fund raiser.

Remember your staff. When I think of all the people who have helped me beyond a reasonable expectation, I wonder if I deserve any credit at all. Chief among these wonderful people are the secretaries and office staff.

In Jefferson City, Elsie Irvin, then office manager, saved me so many times when I needed letters to go out, a report typed, supplies, information from another department, etc., etc. She was so busy but always had time for a friendly smile and getting my work done somehow.

Marian Korsgaard in Chicago, would only work three days per week, but I decided it was better to have her three days than anybody full time (my successor learned about that the hard way). My favorite way to work was to dictate a letter or proposal, revise and have it typed again, sometimes twice again. Marian did not mind that I didn't get it 100 percent right the first time. She remembered things for me when I became preoccupied with an interview or a lengthy report. She knew where everything was, even the things on my desk I had said I would take care of. She didn't waste time visiting too much with other staff, but knew everyone and could easily get the cooperation we often needed. For example, Marian helped me see how invaluable the cashiers could be. They handled all incoming gifts. Each day they told me about gifts from people I had called on in various cities. In spite of the fact that I worked on *deferred* gifts, the *cash* gifts from those I contacted exceeded my total operating costs. That helped with the Finance Committee.

Marian's pleasant personality and interest in her work made each day a happy experience for me. I meant to tell her all this—and started to a few times—but what I said was always inadequate.

Helen Meyers, at Topeka, knew everything about the Foundation and saved me from many mistakes.

Two secretaries at Columbia College I encouraged to move up to a higher position. Helen Grim became a secretarial training teacher and Sue Gunn became Director of Marketing for Advent Enterprises. Sue especially impressed me with her warmth and personality on the phone and in greeting visitors to our office. That, with organizational ability, continues to contribute to her success. I strongly feel that much more should be done to make advancement and recognition possible for secretaries.

There were more marvelous secretaries and I admire all of them, especially for their fortitude in putting up with me.

In a college, the alumni director is invaluable in cultivation. Jane Crow is one such director I have known. And taking my own advice, I'm thanking her now.

Know your limitations—and your strengths. Should you employ a consulting firm to help you get big gifts? You can only answer this if you truly know your strengths and weaknesses. Some examples follow of when you might wish to turn to outside help, or how to know if you need it.

When to consult. Consulting ads have tremendous appeal. You need money desperately, but lack the funds to conduct an effective campaign. Your efforts meet with constant frustrations and disappointments. Here are some examples of what you might see.

* * *

You read that MCM Financial promises "Immediate Funds for Current Operations and Bankable Endowment in Only Five Years." All your problems solved.

* * *

Foundations, and sometimes corporations can be so fussy about proposal requirements, but you lack time to study the guidance instructions and adjust to each set of rules. At this point, turn to something like, *"Preparation of Presentations to Foundations and Corporations,"* a publication offered by Ketchum, Inc., a highly respected firm.

* * *

Your best-ever trust deal is held up by an attorney who doesn't want to take the time to research and prepare an unfamiliar document, a charitable remainder trust. Or, an attorney tells his client, "Don't give your money away. You might need it." Do you suspect he means, "Keep your estate intact, so I can get my full cut when you die." Just as you are realizing how big a problem attorneys can be, you read Sharpe's offer of *"Working with Donors' Attorneys."*

* * *

Do you fear that you should be using computers or using them better? Epsilon will "show you the 'big picture' such as" gift and pledge sourcing, promotional tracking, lapsed donor analysis, direct mail analysis, geodemographic overlays.

* * *

"Computerize your fund-raising research and record keeping with The Grant Seeker."

* * *

The Donald Campbell Co. ads remind me of the wise advice I had from Don himself in the days when we were both launching development careers.

* * *

American City Bureau claims "an unparalleled record of SUCCESS." Thanks for your good pointers when I was starting out. I hear you continue to be a great resource for new development people.

* * *

Mail Management Group will provide over 250 analysis routines to examine your direct mail fund raising.

* * *

Haney Associates properly emphasize feasibility studies "that scrutinize every aspect of the proposed campaign goal." Fine! Careful advance studies are very important.

* * *

Kennedy Sinclaire offers solicitor training programs (a vast potential for improvement here).

* * *

The consultant ads open a wonderland where all your problems are solved, even some you are not yet aware of. Terrific!

Perhaps you think some of them are overselling. Maybe, but I believe the right firm can help you tremendously. But how do you know which one? The answer is know what you know as well as what you don't know. Seek referrals for consultants in the areas you need (*How to Hire the Right Fund Raising Consultant* by Arthur Raybin is an excellent resource). Then seek out opportunities to learn.

Schools and seminars. By the time I had attended several schools by the Philanthropy Tax Institute, Kennedy Sinclaire, Pentera, etc., seminars by CASE, NSFRE, NAHD, read all the books I could find on development, and had some work experience—I felt less need for consultant help.

HOW LEADERSHIP WORKS

Who is the leader? Not only the president or the executive director or the head of fund raising—the leader's special qualities are needed by anyone trying to get volunteers and staff to work, striving to enthuse prospects. What follows are leadership examples that have been helpful to me.

My first development job was with the Kansas City Art Institute. The president was a painter by profession. His oils were much admired. He also had strong leadership qualities.

The dramatic goal. He supplied the picture—the vision—of a college with dormitories, library, cafeteria, art gallery and properly lighted studios. He saw the school fully accredited, attracting students from all over the country. He projected that image so strongly that board members and donors believed it.

He inspired me and the volunteer leadership to provide the nuts and bolts: plans, working drawings, money, supervision. We converted a small art school into a regionally known and well-equipped college in three years. Vision did it.

When I looked at the inadequate, rundown facilities of the Institute in 1961, while hearing Andrew Morgan describe how he visualized it, I was reminded of Thomas J. Watson, Sr. telling how he took over the company that was to become IBM with only 400 employees. Both leaders projected a powerful vision; then things began to happen.

I've been in the office of Thomas J. Watson, Sr., a spacious, quiet place in which to relax and think big. I saw it as a haven to dream up plans for subordinates to carry out, but T.J. didn't operate that way.

He constantly visited plants, laboratories, branch offices, company picnics, and employee dinners. Every employee had the opportunity to shake hands and say a word or two.

I wondered if he didn't tire of being with his people and with his customers so much. Why didn't he retreat to that beautiful office and enjoy the fruits of success? Because he was a leader who must be with his people so he could let them know how important they were, so he could share his vision of a great IBM.

The sisters of Saint Marys Hospital, Mayo Clinic complex, are as intense and enthusiastic as T. J. Watson was. They provide a special quality of service that patients remember forever. Some patients return the love they've received with substantial gifts.

Make the work fun. "What did you find exciting today?" Tom Babb would ask. He wouldn't question how much money I had brought into the American Cancer Society that day, but what I had found interesting and enjoyable. He wanted some fun in the work. In a meeting, Tom would ask, "Who was just elected president of the national society?" He wanted to be sure we all felt part of the national organization.

Listen—and talk when needed. Jerry Quick allowed me free reign to develop my program to fit the situation in Missouri. This included tolerance of mistakes, like the time I paid a lawyer to draw up a trust agreement for a lady who, it turned out, had no intention of making any kind of charitable gift.

I am grateful that Dr. Roy Menninger insisted that I spend three months studying The Menninger Foundation when I began work there. It was a tremendous educational experience, from which I benefit constantly. I didn't think I would need time in all the departments, but he was right. This training proved invaluable in presenting the many operations of The Foundation.

If your boss seems less enthusiastic about you and your work than you think is appropriate, check it out.

I had two or three instances of this, but did nothing because I thought my reports showed I was doing a good job and answered any questions anyone might have. I didn't realize how many reports and other things the boss had.

I should have made an appointment for a frank and heart-to-heart talk about how I was doing. The problems the boss was concerned about were misunderstandings and could easily have been cleared up if he or I would have had initiated a friendly talk. Unfortunately, I discovered this too late, for that boss.

Once I learned the importance of an informal talk with the top man once in a while, both of us enjoyed the experience. Being boss is a lonely job.

Good management encourages everyone to help locate prospects. The team effort inspired by Graham Clark and Stephen Jennings at the School of The Ozarks pays off constantly. One example is the Florida couple who just executed their eighth gift annuity and the story was fully reported in the newsletter.

My wife, Betty, retired as secretary of our medium-size church. She often brought work home, stayed late, went in early, and worked weekends to get paperwork done. Why? Because she was always taking extra time and with people who phoned or came in.

She was intent on helping people as much as possible, just like the excellent leaders. Intensity. An image of the church as caring. Attention to detail. People-oriented.

Frank Boyden started the Deerfield Academy in western Massachusetts with fourteen boys in 1902. His office consisted mainly of a card table just inside the main entrance.

For his first sixty years, he personally gave every grade to every student. Each boy had a private talk with the headmaster six times a year and was told where he stood. Boyden met with all 500 students as a group daily.

Along with such extraordinary attention to his students, he wrote seventy letters daily, and spent huge amounts of time in the community and with the colleges which his graduates attended. If you have such a wonderful leader, he will generate stories you can tell in your talks or put in your letters and proposals. A great way to build confidence in your leadership.

Help others achieve. The fund raiser is helpless without good people to work with him. Two of the most important are the top volunteer leader and the chief executive officer. Let's call them your board chairman and your president. If you are evaluating a job (either to accept one or to stay in the one you have)—please recognize how much these two have to do with your future. They are the key to enlisting effective helpers. They can block you or encourage you to success.

The president represents what you are selling. In fact, *you are selling him.* My first president was a painter. That won him recognition in artistic circles and, with the faculty, this ability earned him respect and excellent working relationships. He also knew everything going on in the college from maintenance to academic programs, from student activities to library needs. He participated with his students in both fun and learning experiences. As a good administrator, he provided a saleable product: exciting education for a growing body of students. He gave me what I had to have and it didn't matter that he declined to have anything to do with fund raising. When I mentioned that the board should be more active, he said, "You handle it." Fine.

Transformation of the board. I went to our board chairman with the records of activity and giving, almost completely negative for many members. Some were wealthy and important, big factors in other charities. But they didn't even attend our board meetings. Why? I was told that they had originally been asked just to "lend their names." That is all they did. We decided to visit each board member to present the need for both gifts and work. An interview would go like this, "Charlie and I stopped by to brief you on the new programs approved by the board." After describing projects and costs, "We must first look to the board for financial support and we are here to ask for yours." We were prepared to ask for a specific amount if appropriate, to urge attendance at meetings, and to offer a definite work assignment to fit his qualifications.

They listened and some made more or less affirmative responses. Those who failed to produce contributions or volunteer participation were elevated to "honorary trustee." We made another visit to each to present a recognition plaque. Some later became contributors.

Then the real work began. We recruited trustees who were told what was expected and who agreed to put money and effort into the school. One new trustee in particular proved to be a great leader in philanthropic giving and so his family continues to this day.

In addition to a weak board, this is what we started with: no dormitories, no accreditation, little regional and no national recognition, inadequate facilities, and finances so uncertain it was sometimes thought the school would go under. In just under three years, with powerful board leadership, the following was achieved:

1. Two dormitories, a library, cafeteria, and art gallery built.
2. Accreditation achieved.
3. Publicity gained (one-hour TV documentary, many newspaper stories, TV interviews, famous visiting speakers and artists).
4. Number of students increased, with market range extended to many states.
5. Momentum continued to the present day, over twenty years. New buildings were added recently as proof that the college does well and continues to meet an important need.

Someone who knew this history might exclaim, "Hey Charlie, don't forget that big bequest which put the campaign over the top. You lucked out." Yes, that was the largest gift and was a factor to put this little college into sound financial condition. But it wasn't just a stroke of luck. The trustee who gave us that legacy had strong opinions about education and we spent a lot of time with him, discussing his ideas. For example, he liked traditional art and we got together special exhibitions mainly for his benefit. A lot of work for a gift, but it paid off. I saw what cultivation can accomplish for financial support and have believed in it ever since.

I hope this story demonstrates the importance of the president who made sure the programs were excellent and that the school was worth selling. He inspired confidence in me, in the staff, and in the donors. It also illustrates the courage and energy of the board chairman. He took a lot of time from his business. More important, he ran the risk of offending prominent people in his home town where he had to do business, and to see socially these same people. But he handled it well. No one was offended to be elevated to "honorary." Also, no one objected to being asked to give more than any board member had given before. He presented the facts in a pleasant, convincing manner. As a fairly young man, this was his first major philanthropic undertaking. His achievement of such a remarkable turnaround was the beginning of a series of accomplishments which have earned Byron Shutz an enviable reputation.

I was lucky to work with these two men in my first development job. My suggestion to you: Don't rely on luck. Take a good look before you accept a new job or decide to stay another year where you are.

I have turned down consulting jobs when it became apparent the board and the staff leadership expected me to produce the funds by some kind of magic without effort on their part. If you find such a situation, you may convert such people to doers. Or you might do better to walk away.

One of my pleasures is to recall working for William Scarborough, president of Baker University. Always willing to go with me on a prospect call, his friendliness and persuasive powers carried conviction. Rather than take the spotlight himself, he often pushed me into making the principal presentation at an alumni or board meeting. That was to develop my abilities and confidence. Moreover, he sent me in his place to make important talks. Bill made me feel in full partnership with him to do our very best for Baker.

Find such a leader and your success will be assured.

USE PAPERWORK EFFECTIVELY

It is a good idea to operate under a set of guidelines, approved by your board.

Guidelines can define items such as:

1. Use of legal counsel.
2. Description of gift plans you offer.
3. Who will approve and sign agreements.
4. May your organization act as trustee?
5. Obligations to the donor.
   Make sure that donor has sufficient funds remaining for his use and for the natural objects of his bounty.
   Avoid conflict of interest.
   Be sure donor consults his own legal advisors.
6. Records.
7. Continuing education of staff and volunteers.

You need the backing of your board and of your top executives. You will have it (and in writing), if all understand and approve your guidelines as to designated responsibilities.

This is an example of an important point to cover: when you accept a charitable gift annuity, you create a potential obligation for your organization. This should be clearly stated in your guidelines so that no one has a surprise waiting.

Regular reports are a must. Reports to your chief executive, governing board, and volunteer committees are necessary. What should you include? Did you get results? Your main objective is to answer that question.

I believe it usually takes three years to show results from a new deferred giving program. So, after almost four years, I presented proof of that to the American Cancer Society, Illinois Division for the first four years of the new program:

Bequest and Trust Receipts

Beginning Year:	$1,731,063
Second Year:	2,359,527
Third Year:	2,129,675
Fourth Year:	2,800,000 (approx.)

In the American Cancer Society, much of the work is done through volunteers. So, I reported on who we were recruiting and training. I described their qualifications. Board members were reassured that we had bank presidents, prominent attorneys, heads of trust departments, and social leaders representing the Society. I presented the materials being supplied to our volunteers.

Your reports will also describe seminars, special gifts, workshops, and training meetings. They will present analyses of your mailing results and could include the numbers and types of contacts you have made. For example, since most people do not understand what a development officer does, I generally try to show the various aspects of the work. Once, I recorded my inquiry and prospect contacts for a year (working five to ten days per month):

Phone	204
Letters	155
Proposals	28
Personal Calls	113
Calls Assigned to Volunteers	43

Reports can also define expectations. Estimate how much money you will raise and when. Define major objectives such as improving mailing lists, developing a speakers' bureau, etc.

Reports from volunteers. Incorporate statements from your volunteers. Fig. 9-1 is one such statement I passed out at workshops.

Tell the boss what you do. Something unusual in the way of a report to my boss was called "Sample of Prospect Calls." This resulted from some problems.

I experienced a failure of communication with two bosses. In one case I tried to get him to speak to alumni groups and to make calls with me. One call was for setting up a $1 million land trust. He was incensed that I wanted him to make that trip (there was a health reason why he preferred to stay home which I later heard about).

The other had little idea of long-range cultivation and especially not of how the president should help get major gifts. He seemed to be more disapproving than helpful.

One day I began to think how *I* could prevent such a problem. Since then, I have enjoyed excellent communication and understanding with my bosses. It may be due, in part, to the reports I have prepared on my own initiative such as a brief history of prospect calls. Examples (details omitted) from one report log:

> A land gift of $75,000 in Jefferson City, with strings attached. Procedure to close.
>
> Obtained requested information for a Joplin prospect, will name American Cancer Society in his will.
>
> A volunteer chairman has named the American Cancer Society in his will and also has a client who has designated "residue to the American Cancer Society."
>
> Major philanthropist in Kansas City has included American Cancer Society in his charitable trust.
>
> Progress on a unitrust with about $70,000 going to the American Cancer Society.
>
> St. Louis inquiry resulted in interest in unitrusts, for $50,000 to start and later additions of $550,000.
>
> Advanced cultivation of a radio-TV owner by proposal for a $10,000 gift annuity.
>
> Bank vice-president has two clients who have established bequest provisions for the American Cancer Society.
>
> Progress on two $80,000 annuity trusts.
>
> Volunteer attorney has client making $45,000 bequest to the American Cancer Society.

Records can be of great help. Record keeping must also receive serious attention. The Menninger Foundation has the best files I have ever seen or imagined. Spend two or three hours in study of one of those files and your preparation for gathering additional background is superb.

My favorite duty is not working on reports, instructions, or paperwork. But it is absolutely necessary. Do it well.

Report preparation helps you face the facts of where you are and to make realistic plans. The more others understand your program, problems, and progress—the greater chance they will join with you in your achievements.

Training manual. Instruction manuals are widely used. It takes a lot of time to prepare one and more time to review with those who should use it. My guess is that this great amount of time would be better spent before good prospects. However, when brief, training manuals can be excellent tools and serve the same purpose as guidelines. If you need a training manual, here is an outline:

Purpose
Organization Structure
Requirements for Volunteers
Leadership
Committee Responsibilities
Staff Training
Calendar
Publicity
Meetings and Seminars
Sample Letters
Certificates and Awards
Action Plan
Achievement Report

Fig 9–1. *Statement for a volunteer on special gifts**

I. **Objective:**
The Special Gifts effort seeks to persuade individuals, companies, and foundations to consider the importance of winning the battle against cancer by giving *in proportion* to the *size* of the problem and *their own financial ability to give.*

II. **Definition:**
A Special Gift is one that has been received from a donor which was the result of a planned approach by a special gift organization. It usually includes one or more personal calls.

III. **Prospects:**
All *individuals, corporations, corporate and individual foundations,* and *trusts* from whom sizeable gifts may be expected and to whom a specially planned, personal approach is made.

The general appeal to wipe out cancer is sufficient to obtain a great many donors of small amounts through the Residential and Employee solicitations, but in order to get larger amounts the appeal must be made by special contacts to the larger potential donors. It is well to remember, particularly in the field of Special Gifts, that people give to people, not necessarily to causes and by combining the right person and the universal desire to conquer cancer we have an unbeatable combination.

A. Special gift prospects may be found in a number of sources.
   1. Generous memorial contributors
   2. Generous past contributors
   3. Prominent persons
   4. Community leaders
   5. Newspapers
   6. Wealthy retired persons
   7. Patron lists
   8. Corporation boards and executives
   9. Chamber of Commerce

B. Special Gift contributors need year-round attention if their maximum interest is to be retained for any length of time. This is called *cultivation.* It is easy enough to take a person's money, but it is a little more difficult to keep in regular touch with each Special Giver.

   Cultivation can and should be done using the following techniques:
   1. Newsletter
   2. Annual Report
   3. Corporate Gift letter and brochure
   4. Corporate Budget brochure
   5. Announcements
   6. Meetings
   7. Program Activities

IV. **Organization:**
Proper organization and planning is the key to a successful Special Gift Crusade.

The General Crusade Chairman is charged with the responsibility of recruiting a Special Gift Chairman. The Special Chairman should be a top man in the community from a financial viewpoint and he, himself, should be a Special Giver *if he expects to lead others in the same direction.*

Presented at the Annual Meeting of the American Cancer Society, by Gene Bradley of Kansas City.

Chapter 10

KNOW WHEN TOO MUCH REALLY ISN'T

Deferred giving is the lowest cost per dollar raised. You can document this from any organization with a supportive public and a ten-year program that has been effective and consistent. Avoid looking at the start-and-stops and those who refused necessities such as good literature, well-planned mailings, personal cultivation, and competent staff.

The money that eventually comes in is tremendous, yet those who hold the purse strings are often reluctant to fund the program to get it going. Development offices, faced with what seems an enormous task, put off starting a program. Don't fall into these traps.

Making the case. Joseph S. Rogers, California attorney, is a volunteer expert. For more than twenty-five years, he was primarily responsible for major gift cultivation in the California division of the American Cancer Society. He said that their cost of legacy promotion was 1.5 cents for every dollar raised.

Their office (when I was there some years ago) had 1,100 files of current and future bequests, averaging $12,000 each. That indicated annual receipts from trusts and legacies of more than $8 million. For some years it has been much more. Rogers pointed out a ten-year period during which legacy income increased more than 400 percent.

He explained that promotion yields more per dollar spent in developing major gifts than in any other area. This is also the most neglected program, he added. While most development people are sold on the need for special gift promotion efforts, such are difficult to begin and a problem to keep going.

Two out of ten or one out of two? In general fund raising, I have found that about two out of ten calls prove to be productive beyond nominal or courtesy gifts. However, Dartmouth College established that in the deferred giving area of promotion, one out of two calls resulted in benefits to the college, often substantial.

Dartmouth also discovered that the first several years of promotion did not show increases in trust and bequest gifts. But, after eight years, the increases were spectacular. It takes at least some years for the promotion to show results.

The Illinois Division of the American Cancer Society showed an increase of $1 million per year in the fourth year of a new promotion program. Cost of operation ranged from less than 1 percent to 1.5 percent. Persistence with a sound procedure pays off.

I traveled to some small towns in Illinois for Columbia College. The resultant outright gifts amounted to three times the cost of the trip. Then, a few years later, the college announced it had received the largest gift in its history. It was a bequest from a lady I had seen on one of those Illinois calls. She was pleasant, but I had picked up no hint that she would ever make such a large gift. That call made the trip exceptionally cost-effective.

Can we afford it? "But we can't afford it!" is sometimes a board member's comment. The development director feels like replying, "You mean we cannot afford to spend $50,000 to bring in $500,000?" Figuring in all kinds of overhead, there is still a net profit of more than $400,000.

The board member may exclaim, "But we will have to wait for the money. A bequest provision may not pay off for many years." He's probably thinking that his term is up in a year or two and he wants results now—while he is still on the board. O.K., give him what he wants. Include outright major gifts in your promotion. If you are spending $50,000, plan to raise at least $100,000 in outright gifts. The bequests and trust payments due in future years are extra.

For the price of afternoon tea. The outright gift leads to the deferred gift. When this lady's name was given to me, I could not find her in the phone book. So I wrote to her that I would be staying at the Bel-Air (chosen because of past and hoped-for-gifts from the owner, who lived next door) and that I would like to see her but did not have her phone number.

Upon my arrival, the desk clerk handed me a message that her chauffeur had delivered. It contained her unlisted phone number. She liked the Bel-Air because it was close to her home and she would speak with me in its lobby.

On subsequent trips, I had many visits with her in the Beverly Hilton since it was even closer to her home. There were plenty of quiet, pleasant corners in the spacious lobby, and we enjoyed a snack in the colorful coffee shop.

Afternoon tea with her always resulted in a $5,000 check

within a week or two. She mostly discussed problems concerning her daughter and her servants. She didn't want to talk at home because her German cook listened.

Only once did I mention anything about a gift to The Menninger Foundation. This angered her and she sent only $1,000. I took the hint: my role was to be a good listener. The cost of the cultivation dropped to almost nothing considering the annual gifts and her bequest.

The inexpensive, "expensive" lunch. At her class reunion, an alumna from New Orleans said she would like to talk to me about her will, that she would like to leave something to her college. On my next trip to New Orleans, I found she was a secretary who no longer worked much due to illness. She appeared to live modestly.

When I invited her to lunch at Brennan's, she was delighted. We had turtle soup, trout amandine, two or three slices of French bread, and praline sundae. She relaxed and discussed her plans.

After our first lunch, she named her alma mater in her will. After each lunch thereafter, she decided on a larger share. Finally, she announced we would receive all, since her relatives were already rich.

As she told me more about her situation over the years, I realized her means were limited and her earning power minimal. I began to wonder if her generosity in increasing the bequest meant anything. I did not understand why her will was so important to her.

At our last lunch, before I moved to another position, she explained everything. She would soon inherit from three rich relatives who were elderly and ill. This part-time secretary, who had to count the pennies all her life, expected to die a wealthy woman. She might accomplish more by her will than she had achieved in her whole life. Sometimes I questioned the wisdom of spending college money on those lunches, but now I realize that could be the most important thing I did for the college.

I chose to relate this example because I suspect there may be some who believe that lunch at Brennan's twice a year was primarily for the pleasure of the fund raiser. O.K., it is nice to enjoy one's work. If some fringe benefits go with the job, all the better. But from the college point of view, what was it worth to become sole beneficiary in that will? And was there a better way to achieve such a result?

Chapter 11

TELL THE MANAGEMENT STORY—INSPIRE AND MOTIVATE

As I have written throughout this book in various ways, a key to success in getting the major gifts is to find the motivation to inspire the prospect to become a donor. Although I have focused on the prospect and donor up to this point, a complete fund-raising program turns this key to success on the staff as well. Good management, properly told and applauded, can serve to inspire both the prospect and your staff to new heights.

TELL YOUR PROSPECTS

Most people of wealth consider themselves hardheaded business managers who hesitate to entrust a major gift to persons who may be labeled impractical idealists. Maybe potential donors perceive your college as being run by professors with little experience in practical affairs. Don't jump up to tell me that is wrong and what modern management practices you follow. Tell your prospects. They may be surprised to learn how little staff you have and how efficiently you use each gift.

Tell how good your management is. Why are major donors sometimes so interested in a personal interview with your president? Or the prospect may say nothing, but the gift does not happen until contact from your top executive. The donor wants to be assured by the person in charge that his money will be well handled. He wishes to demonstrate his own good judgment in selecting the charity, and that he has verified the ability of management. So why not say some things about management in your presentations?

Nonprofits have made great advances in various management areas, such as improved yields in investments, mailing list tests, effectiveness of case statements, quality and readability of brochures and in construction designs of buildings. However, you might take a look at what your big business donors are reading. What aspects of management are now up for examination? I heard many comments about *In Search of Excellence* by Tom Peters and Robert H. Waterman, Jr. (see Appendix). It stirred up some deep thinking about better ways to manage. Now, *A Passion for Excellence* by Tom Peters and Nancy Austin has helped generate still more seminars, video and audio cassettes, and a flood of ideas on how to improve management. The authors of these books claim that "a revolution is on, that managers in every field are rethinking . . . the principles that often have served their institutions poorly . . . all are searching." They point to the need for leadership "unleashing energy, building, freeing and growing."

I am referring to just two of the books, but there are more that treat the new ways of improving management.

TELL YOUR STAFF

Do you encourage innovation? Is your organization going in for decentralization to develop initiative by smaller groups? Are your people encouraged to be innovative to the fullest and to rejoice in their own achievements? If you work for a hospital, is helping the patient get well almost an obsession with *all* staff? Do staff and volunteers feel *ownership* in your organization? Are small victories encouraged with exciting recognition? The new leaders apply such concepts in amazing ways and the books show how well they work.

The excellent leader inspires to a powerful degree. Dr. Howard Johnson, the former president of MIT, said that great leaders have "a visceral form of spiritual energy." They have a picture of the goal, demonstrate enormous attention to detail and project empathy. Vitality and drive are always evident.

Are your leaders out selling? Do your top managers take five names and report on them in the campaigns? Do they call, in person, on each VIP (very important prospect)? Selling is their biggest job, so how much time do they spend doing it? Do they rely on numbers and printouts and lose the feel of the people who will make or break the organization?

Work on the line for a day. A health director in Pennsylvania sent supervisory people out to work in service bureaus four hours per week to answer complaints, fill out forms, and experience what the problems are in the front line. They discovered unnecessary work and some well-justified complaints and suggestions that would otherwise have remained buried.

None of the above may apply to your boss, but think of the great innovative programs he *is* carrying out and write a story for your people.

Tell success stories. I made a training presentation to the Missouri employees of the American Cancer Society that described how to operate a deferred giving program. The package came from the national office and included plenty of slides and handout materials. This was followed by a volunteer who told how he did what I was describing. His talk was received with much more interest and enthusiasm. I didn't understand the significance of that until reading Tom Peters and Nancy Austin who say to throw away the manuals that dictate—that ram down the throat. They say to present success stories. When Myron Sildon got up and told step-by-step how he obtained major gifts in Kansas City, that was far more stimulating to action than all my charts, procedure steps, and statistics.

If the success story works so well in training, why not also use its dramatic power in proposals?

Focus your efforts. Think about what is the most important thing your organization does. Do you provide education for students, care for patients? Do you symbolize your concern by paying obsessive attention to that? Peters and Austin say that "the remarkable cleanliness of Disney's parks is merely a matter of a lot of people trying to do cleanliness better." Somebody thought about not selling gum and a thousand people thought of more such ideas to keep the parks super-clean. Dramatize how your people concentrate on your main objective.

Avoid bureaucracy. Church denominations, large health organizations, huge universities, and enormous hospitals tend to become bureaucratic and sluggish. When a problem arises, the solution is to appoint a committee or to form a task force. The new thinking is to cut down on bureaucracy. One way is to give the responsibility to one individual who has complete freedom to ask for help up and down the line and to take responsibility for action.

Has your organization gone beyond so much dependence on formal groups, lengthy reports, and blind following of approved procedures? Do you encourage commitment, enthusiasm, and suggestions from everyone? If so, tell about it.

In making surveys of paperwork procedures in the home

offices of insurance companies, I found clerks on the line had the best ideas for improvements. This amazed the bosses. It shouldn't have. They should have been listening all the time. In fact, they should have been in the work areas helping do the work for a day or two once in a while. Do you have a boss who keeps in touch with what is actually going on? An interesting item to tuck in your proposal.

Prove your management. Perhaps you have a story to tell about how you achieve remarkable results with a lean staff. Great! Your potential donors will listen with enthusiasm.

If you have a donor who should be ready to come through with that big gift but hesitates for unknown reasons, find a way to convince him of how effectively you use each dollar contributed. Take your boss or top volunteer leader along on the call, find a dramatic story to show results from past gifts, and zero in on the special interests of the donor to personalize your proposal. Include in your presentation a way to prove your excellent management. It may produce a solid "Yes!"

Chapter 12

USE VOLUNTEERS

Volunteers offer a way to multiply the range and effectiveness of your efforts.

The National Fund Raiser said in April 1986, that volunteers invest six billion work hours each year in helping nonprofit groups. They would receive one out of four dollars raised—if paid.

Volunteers can reduce overhead.

Some of my friends in the business say, "You cannot rely on volunteers to obtain major gifts." But Dartmouth and other colleges have had excellent results from volunteer committees, especially in locating prospects and in accomplishing certain stages of the cultivation process.

A VOLUNTEER SOLICITATION COMMITTEE

If you are seeking 100 gifts of $1,000 or more, with emphasis on over $5,000—you will organize volunteers to contact 300 to 400 prospects. This will require sixty to eighty volunteers.

Structure. The chairman should be a prominent citizen of stature who will make a gift himself and will identify prospects.

Committee members should be community leaders such as company presidents, marketing executives, attorneys, C.P.A. tax specialists, social leaders, etc.

Each volunteer should have five prospects to cultivate as required during the year. The best is when you can get a volunteer to undertake a cultivation program over several years.

Many qualified prospects are not now significant donors. However, we should give special attention to $500-and-up donors. Some organizations will set this figure at $100 and up, others $1,000 and up, etc.

Based on knowledge of the community, project both an average gift amount and the number of gifts required based on the average gift amount, to reach the goal. Next, calculate the number of prospects it will be necessary to visit in order to achieve the required number of gifts. (Rule of thumb: three or four calls are required for each success among inexperienced volunteers; prestige volunteers, experienced in solicitation, may enjoy a success rate of almost 100 percent.) Then, based on a ratio of one solicitation volunteer for every five prospects, calculate the number of Solicitation Volunteers.

Solicitation Volunteer qualifications. There are certain qualifications which are the prerequisites to an individual's success. Recruitment of individuals possessing these qualifications will be absolutely essential if the effort expended on the program is not to be wasted. These qualifications are:

1) Annual income comparable to that of prospects.
2) Influence in the community.
3) Willingness to make a personal contribution or pledge first.

Captains. If implementation of the program requires more than five Solicitation Volunteers, one or more levels of leadership in addition to the Chairman will be required in order to recruit the necessary number of Solicitors. Once again, the number required can be determined by using a ratio of one recruiter to every five "recruitees." For example, if it has been determined that 100 calls will be necessary to reach the goal, the Chairman will want to recruit four Captains, who in turn will recruit five Solicitation Volunteers each, for a total of twenty Solicitation Volunteers. These twenty Solicitors will in turn call on five prospects apiece, for a total of 100 calls.

Responsibilities. The committee should develop, in conjunction with staff director,

- Objectives
- Timetable
- Publicity
- Record-keeping system
- Speakers' bureau
- Recognition for donors

The most important activity is deciding on a list of prospects and organizing personal calls by committee members. Letters before and after the calls are important. The prospects are often the same as those who should be solicited for major annual gifts. It is sometimes a good idea to combine special gift with legacy promotion.

The very *best* prospects are those with assets of over $500,000, volunteers, past donors, singles or couples with no children, age fifty and up, family foundations, etc. However, you will always include some for special reasons.

Certain events will trigger the desire or the ability to give such as: special need for your services, inheritance, good business profit, sales of land, before a trip, retirement approaching, etc.

Present plans to the board of directors once a year.

The committee should undertake special mailings to particular groups such as attorneys, trust officers, C.P.A.s, chartered life underwriters, etc. to keep them informed of programs, correct legal name and planned gifts offered so they will be in a position to describe the opportunity of a bequest or trust provisions when the occasion develops.

Safeguard confidential information.

As to inquiries from mailings, local mailings, or individual contacts: mail materials requested, follow up two weeks later, find out the prospect's special interest, make a written record. Develop a cultivation plan.

SELECTING THE RIGHT VOLUNTEER

Look for volunteers especially qualified for working with certain groups. For example, find a physician to contact others in the medical profession with an appeal aimed at successful doctors.

The president of the American Cancer Society in a certain state at one time was a specialist in cancer surgery—capable, highly respected, wealthy. But he gave no money to the Society. His wife was asked about this and replied, "He gives his time which is very valuable. Why should he give money?"

The answer was a deferred gift annuity with more advantages than listing as a charitable donor:

1. Immediate charitable deduction.
2. Future income, partly tax-free.
3. Reduction of management and investment worries.
4. Possible savings in probate costs and estate taxes.

The major financial objective of many doctors is to provide for retirement, and, in some cases, to provide generously for their hospitals, medical schools, health organizations, or churches. Both personal and charitable objectives can be accomplished with a gift annuity or unitrust. There are many other types of charitable trust plans, but I would build examples on those specific concepts for volunteers to present.

Try to find insurance salesmen who will sell policies naming your charity. I have talked at insurance meetings on charitable gifts as another type of insurance policy to sell. Use the pourover trust as an especially interesting example (life insurance to increase the size of a testamentary trust).

A yacht dealer may know someone who no longer uses his yacht and would welcome a charitable deduction over the bother of trying to sell. The same dealer will sell the yacht for you and tell his fellow dealers. It is important to stay away from the valuation question. Be free to sell for what you can get.

There are many examples of groups, such as real estate brokers and attorneys, in which a highly respected member is your best volunteer.

Exercise caution. There are some cautions regarding volunteers. Sometimes we are so delighted to find someone ready to help, we waste a lot of time before realizing we made a selection mistake. Choose carefully.

Some years ago I started on a new job with a church-related college and found that my predecessor had a campaign all set up. He had captains and workers selected in a particular area as the start of a larger project. He said the organizational and training meetings had been held, supplies distributed, and all was ready for the money to roll in. It was a beautiful way to start a new job—except for one thing. No calls were made and no gifts were obtained. All the captains were ministers who had their own solicitations to think about. The captains did nothing and the workers never started. I found new leaders who were willing to work and it went fine.

Another time I inherited a statewide legacy chairman who agreed to do everything I asked him. But he spent his time selling insurance, not doing anything for the Society. I replaced him as quickly as possible, but not before I had wasted too much time.

In recruiting, get background information *before* you select the leaders and workers who *can* and *will* do the job. Make it very clear what you expect. An easy way to do that is to go over job descriptions in detail with the prospective worker.

TRAINING AND EVALUATION

You select some situations to be presented with discussion of how a volunteer might proceed to develop a gift. These workshops may later be used by each chairman in training his committee.

Your committee should do its own planning—look ahead to determine activities and target dates for the year.

Fig. 12-1 illustrates a sample of what you may work out with them.

A VOLUNTEER SUCCESS STORY

This story is based on an actual person. He was a true philanthropist, generous to the school I worked for, a wonderful volunteer. But he had the means and the interest to do much more in outstanding gifts. I knew enough to ask for money, but had no conception of how to develop a big gift or how to spark his maximum efforts with others. Now, in retrospect, I see how I might have done better—how you can do better.

Easy to get a check. When the school needed money, I explained the situation to John and he wrote a check. The sum looked very big to me, since it was more than most people gave. I was happy and never thought I should do anything more.

Habits of the rich. Sometimes John and I had lunch in the cafeteria across from his office. He said it was quick and cheap. He preferred it to his club which was eight blocks away, slower and more expensive.

John was one of my teachers in investments. He had an office only large enough for plenty of file cabinets, an old desk, and a first-class secretary. He showed me how he tracked prices, economic developments, management changes, etc. for the bonds and stocks he had selected for study. In the last several years he had profits of over $13 million and did no work other than to look after his personal investments.

Despite the economical lunches and frugal office, he lived well in some ways. He spent time doing light work on his farm, in his residence in New York City, relaxing at his Country Club, and in faithful attendance at a variety of board meetings. Since he was not married, his meals, clothes, housecleaning, etc. were supervised by his valet.

He concentrated on his gifts. Charitable gifts were very important and considered as carefully as his investments.

Why did he give so generously to our college? This is embarrassing, but I do not know. I was so intent on getting the checks that I never thought to inquire about motivation.

A development director is busy. I worked hard at my job. Some days I made ten to twenty fund-raising calls myself or with others. I made trips to promote student recruiting. I worked on publicity with newsmen, TV personalties, editors, etc. I developed plans for buildings and new programs. But I should have stopped all that activity for two hours for something more important. I should have called John, asked if we could have lunch, and added: "Let's make it at your club today and take about two hours for a good talk. I want you to tell me in detail why you support our college and what you hope it will accomplish." I believe that John would have been pleased to see that I thought so much of his opinion. Now we get into the fictional projection:

Release of donor power. This meeting revealed that John wanted us to become a nationally famous institution, one of the best. How could this be accomplished? He outlined the items:

1. Higher levels for faculty salaries with emphasis on quality teaching and on attracting two or three big names.
2. A heavily financed lecture series to attract famous people to the campus. Such great achievers, he felt, would build prestige and inspire students.
3. New buildings with the finest equipment.
4. More funds for extensive student recruiting.

I was amazed that a board member had such foresight and such definite plans. The next two months were spent largely in preparing a proposal on the future of the college. Each week or so I reviewed progress with John. We also kept adding names of major gift prospects and who would cultivate them. John presented the final version to the board, announced his own kickoff gift, and asked board members for theirs.

All John needed was encouragement to carry his dreams into reality. Wasn't that more important than most of the things I was so busy with?

Team effort. Of course, others were very much involved. The president was a vital force in the planning and was the major factor in sparking enthusiasm. The board chairman took the lead in obtaining other major gifts. The architect came up with some very attractive ideas. Faculty thought of some tremendous speakers and workshop leaders to invite to campus. John was given an opening to see what could be done—and look what happened!

Your volunteer leaders have the potential for tremendous power. Find out how to give them an opportunity. For more information on managing volunteers, see *The Nine Keys to Successful Volunteer Programs* by Kathleen Fletcher Brown, The Taft Group (Appendix A).

Fig. 12–1. *Suggested volunteer action plan*

ACTIVITY	WHEN TO BE ACCOMPLISHED	BY WHOM
1. Identify, recruit, and train the key volunteers for prospecting and leadership.		
2. Obtain cooperation of resource people such as attorneys, trust officers, C.P.As, investment counselors, insurance estate planners, etc.		
3. Evaluate present mailing list. a. Subtract b. Add		
4. Mail special letters to particular groups such as attorneys, wealthy individuals, etc. Have a person (or persons) with high standing in the group prepare and sign the letters or series of letters and select the most effective enclosure.		
5. Select prospects for personal calls. a. Obtain background information b. Establish purpose		

Fig. 12–1. *Suggested volunteer action plan*

ACTIVITY	WHEN TO BE ACCOMPLISHED	BY WHOM
of call, what to ask for c. Decide who should go d. Set timing		
6. Establish goals.		
7. Recruit additional volunteers both (1) to locate and develop more prospects and (2) to assist with proposal preparation and legal questions.		
8. Set up group participation: a. Training sessions on cultivation of prospects b. Seminars for selected groups c. Invite members of the Committee to speak at service clubs, church groups, etc. d. Schools in Trusts, Estate Planning, New Tax Developments, etc. Have a well-qualified panel, with public invited.		
9. Keep records of activities for the annual report at the end of the year.		

Fig. 12–2. *Achievement report*

TO:

FROM:

Name and Address of Chairman:

Names of Committee Members:

Approximate number of Prospect Names sent for additions to Mailing List: ____________

Approximate number of Mailing List Names Deleted or Corrected: ____________

Number of Local Mailings to Special Groups: ____________

Number of Folders Distributed: __________

Seminars: __________

Publicity Releases: __________

Number of Calls: __________

Talks to Community Groups: __________

Film Showing: __________

Certificate Presentations: __________

Other:____

____

____

____

Fig 12–3. *Job description for a major gift committee member*

- A professional, such as a leading probate attorney, trust officer, tax consultant, or bank president.
- A resource person to locate and evaluate prospects and especially to develop proposals.
- A person of wealth and position, such as the president of an important company or member of a leading family; someone who knows wealthy people and who can and will make prospect calls.

Fig. 12–4. *Job description for chairman of a major gift committee*

- A person of influence and power in the community.
- Someone able and willing to participate in the program with a bequest, large gift, a trust gift, or a life insurance policy.
- A worker, someone who will:
  —Recruit committee members, keep them informed and inspire them to do a good job.
  —Approach very important prospects personally (effective personal calls are absolutely vital to success).
  —Liaison with other chairmen and staff.

Fig. 12–5. *Job description for staff volunteer committee director*

- Individuals who will:
  —Provide policy guidance to the Committee.
  —Assist in the identification, recruitment and training of Committee members.
  —Conduct preliminary prospect research.
  —Provide materials and clerical services required by the program.
  —Coordinate with Committee Chairman the assignments of Committee members for personal contact with individual prospects and various projects including presentation to local groups.

Chapter 13

BECOME A SUCCESSFUL FUND RAISER

I have often tried to be humorous in response to the frequent question: "How can you ask for money?", by replying that I have lots of job security: like the garbage man—nobody wants my job. That is a lie. Fund raisers make themselves targets for the people who do not like to be asked to give and have about as much job security as a college president who likes to tell off his board. And other people do envy some of the fringe benefits. Notice the comments when you leave in the winter for fourteen-hour work days, important calls and meetings in Florida, Arizona, and California.

So how can someone become a successful fund raiser? My story may not be typical (whose is?), but it may give you some clues.

ONE MAN'S PATH

These are the qualifications which helped me most:

1. Interview techniques learned as a credit reporter, counterintelligence special agent, and data-processing salesman.
2. Survey methods practiced in developing proposals for office procedures.
3. Writing ability improved in getting a master's degree in English.
4. Recruiting, organizing, and training volunteers related to executive experience.
5. Public speaking. I happen to have some natural inclination for this, which meant little in business. Very important in development.

Credit investigation. After military service, I went back to work for Dun & Bradstreet in the same job I had four years before, as a reporter, small salary. But now I was married, had experienced executive responsibilities as an officer—felt the need for advancement and *more money.* Soon I became an instructor or assistant supervisor of thirty reporters travelling in outlying areas. This gave me a chance to work a lot of extra hours at night and on Saturdays, but no more salary. So I remembered friends telling me about IBM, a prosperous and generous company.

Sales. The work at IBM started with eight months of training (longer now). The trainees were bright, eager, and determined to win. Our twenty-five men were the most impressive group I had ever been with. But we kept shrinking. Two or three times a week there would be one less. No explanation. What really bothered me was that many who disappeared seemed to have more ability than I had.

Finally, eight of us were left to go to Endicott, New York for completion of training. No more eliminations.

We got to hear and talk with the great man himself, founder of IBM, Thomas J. Watson, Sr. He always wore coat and tie, even at a picnic. His lovely wife took as much interest in each employee as he did.

Incidentally, I hope this story will also provide some insight into the mores of the rich and powerful, as I happened to encounter them.

Success depends on ideas. I developed an idea of how to use IBM equipment for national Dun & Bradstreet data processing and of how to offer more services to businessmen. One of my fellow students, who had been a customer engineer, very sharp, helped work out the proposed procedures in detail at night after each full day. I turned over the finished proposal to one of my teachers and it went through various hands all the way to New York headquarters and came back in the hands of a senior vice president who called me to a private office for a discussion of my proposal. I entered with a smile expecting some sort of appreciation, but he said: "Your proposal has been carefully studied, but we are going to keep you anyhow." What did that mean? It comes to me now that he may have meant that as a joke. Maybe he thought it would be funny for me to think the proposal brought me to the verge of being fired when in reality his mission was to arrange for me to present the proposal in person in the New York World Headquarters. After the presentation, I heard no more about it for many years until I read in *Dun's Review* a description of the wonderful data processing developed for customers—identical to the system I designed.

Watson was strong on employee recognition. He wanted people to be rewarded for a good idea or for outstanding job performance and to be encouraged to do even better. He also wanted employees to feel a part of the company and to be kept fully informed.

One aspect of this program was a system of paying and recognizing the customer engineers who serviced the machines.

I thought this would apply also to salesmen. Turn in a good idea and be presented with a check for $1,000, maybe $5,000. I was wrong (as of that time).

Invention of a lifetime. The most valuable idea I have ever had, the only really big one, came to absolutely nothing.

With the engineers at one of my customers, Cook Electric Company, Research Division, I worked out a way to take information from magnetic tape used in rockets and transfer it into punched holes in IBM cards and thus make the data available for complete machine processing such as sorting, collating, listing, tabulating, etc. I verified storage of data: 4,000 items per inch—far superior to punched cards. I developed a plan for storage and data retrieval using magnetic tape and sent it to World Headquarters. Never had an answer.

A few years later Remington Rand came out with magnetic tape equipment and forced archrival IBM to try to catch up.

What happened to my tape proposal remained a mystery for many years until I found myself at a dinner in New York seated next to IBM's vice-president for research. Just by way of something to say, I told him this story. He remembered the proposed system very well and was present at the meeting with T. J. Watson when it was evaluated. He described Watson's decision not go ahead as a mistake.

IBM was great! Made the 100% Club year after year, felt I had an important job with a wonderful company and made money. If there was a problem it was me, too independent minded, something of a rebel.

Disaster. One of my new customers experienced a sudden reversal when its manufacturing plant burned, for a total loss with no insurance. The IBM rental contract, naturally, was cancelled. My boss said he should have been warned in advance of the possible cancellation so it could have been prevented. That was the prescribed procedure, to submit a warning report of possible cancellation. What puzzled me was that the cause was the disastrous fire which eliminated the company as a manufacturer, with no way to rebuild. My boss did not explain how I could have advised him the fire would occur or how he would have prevented the fire. Time to move on.

Sales specialization. I landed a good position—Special Representative to Home Office Insurance Companies in the Chicago Area for Addressograph-Multigraph Corporation. This was an advancement above salesman and meant I had more time to research office procedures and to prepare more detailed proposals.

I studied insurance paper work and finally became an expert. My IBM training was invaluable in how to study and survey.

The president of one insurance company said he wanted to consider the possible improvements in his data processing which might be available through new equipment, but he did not want several salesmen coming in taking up his employees' time with surveys which would largely duplicate each other. He asked me to make the survey for all companies and to prepare three proposals for the three best combinations of equipment. He made his decision based on my work and some companies received surprise orders.

At Bankers Life & Casualty Co., I requested permission to survey paperwork procedures and wrote up all thirteen departments in detail. When I brought this book back to the Executive Vice President, Leo Lehane, he said it was the first time anyone had completely described the flow of paperwork in what had just become the second largest casualty insurance company in the United States. Lehane said, "Let's give this a new title," wrote "Office Manual" and called to an aide to put it out to all departments.

John D. MacArthur, sole owner of the company, was by far the richest man I ever got to know well. He taught me much about philanthropy over many years.

When I first started I was often referred to a "Miss Hyland" who occupied a small office on the second floor. The response to an important suggestion for change was usually, "What does Miss Hyland think?" So I began asking her. After about a year I discovered who this formidable lady was, *Mrs.* John D. MacArthur who worked with him from the time they started the company with a few hundred dollars.

John had a robust enjoyment of many things, but best of all was to see his brother, Charles, ("Front Page" author) in New York and his sister-in-law, Helen Hayes. A great lady, whom Betty and I enjoyed meeting when she was in Chicago doing *Mrs. McThing,* an introduction arranged by one of MacArthur's aides, my good friend, Andy Bostrom.

One day MacArthur walked into the office, arms full of address lists, magazines, and other papers. All of which he dumped on the desk of a supervisor: "This is *Theatre Arts Magazine* which I just bought when I got drunk with Charles in New York. It's been losing money. Make it pay." He did.

Another invention. With our research people in Cleveland I developed a machine to start with a roll of paper direct from the mill, at one end. It cut, printed, punched, and imprinted IBM punched card premium notices ready to mail at the other end—all in one machine. The proposal I prepared for this and related equipment was for the largest amount of money that anyone in my company had ever put in a proposal. It was approved all the way up to MacArthur. At this point I made a mistake. I thought it would be nice to bring my boss, Regional Manager, Ed, out for the conference with MacArthur, so he could share the pleasure of this big order. I said to Ed: "MacArthur is a Scotsman who prides himself on being a trader. He never mades a deal unless he can drive a bargain. We must make some concessions," and I named the items we could give on. But Ed was not impressed with MacArthur's sloppy attire, ordinary-looking office, and lack of respect for anyone as important as the Regional Manager. My boss was adamant, made no concessions and the proposal was not approved. After the meeting, Ed said, "He doesn't have any money," because during the meeting MacArthur told his treasurer, who phoned, to buy some warehouse receipts in the company name "because I don't have any money." Not long after *Fortune Magazine* called him the richest man in Chicago. I finally got all of the order piece-by-piece, but it took three years.

Great days. With the business from these Chicago insurance companies, especially Bankers and Allstate, I became the top salesman and gave a speech at the Greenbriar in White Sulphur Springs as the leading salesman in the United States. The president of the company, Bass Ward, asked me to ride horseback with him each year on those narrow mountain trails which we both enjoyed very much. One time I went ahead to open a gate and had trouble with it. Bass called out, "Put more ass into it!" That was the Bass Ward philosophy of selling.

The several trips to the Greenbriar and lunch with President Bass Ward at his Cleveland country club were great experiences. But the single high point during my business career was at a dinner in Endicott, New York when Thomas J. Watson, Sr., introduced me to Dwight Eisenhower, the man I had worked with and talked with on the telephone in Europe but had never seen.

Such men inspired me to wonder if I was doing as much as possible with my own abilities.

Remembrance of things past. What had happened to the idealism of my youth? What was I achieving with my life? Was my education being used?

Perhaps I could find some type of public service work suited to my abilities, which I would enjoy and which would pay a salary. I would make less than in business and certainly not as much as I might expect to make, having just risen to manager five years before. But that was O.K. I had enough savings to supplement living expenses. I needed some kind of regular income and the dean at Drake University suggested college development. Perfect. The cultivation of major sales in data processing is similar to the development of major gifts, an office to manage in each case, public relations (but from a different angle), and a sales staff (but made up of volunteers).

Much that I had learned could transfer, but at the same time I could find the intellectual atmosphere stimulating, renew my youth through contact with students, and find serenity strolling under the oaks and elms.

A new goal. My venture into a new career is focused on that dull sales meeting in Cedar Rapids. I was sitting with a view of Old Main (typical red brick and ivy covered), and the campus of Coe College across the street, and kept thinking, "I should be there at the college. That is where I belong." The next day, I was in that same Old Main talking to President McCabe about college development, and it seemed right.

After many years in business—the thrill of closing a big order, the pursuit of advancement were not so important. A moment comes when a man remembers old dreams, longs to fulfill himself in a more significant way. Many solve this problem through service clubs, church, chamber of commerce, etc. It was partly by accident that I chose a more drastic step.

I was satisfied as branch manager for a large business machines firm, an outstanding and progressive company. Over the years I had made many friends in the business, the pension plan was good, and I knew the products. However, when the sales manager asked me to transfer to a distant city, I turned down the opportunity because, for family reasons, we could not make a long move at that time. This created an impasse and it seemed a good time to request a leave of absence to take courses at Drake University for a master's degree in English and psychology. At first, this did not seem to be an abrupt change, and I told myself that some months of study would qualify me for a better job with the company. The top men were interested, friendly, and even slightly encouraging. But once the direction of my interests was changed, it became apparent that I was starting a new career in my mid-forties. With my particular company, at least, I believe that going back to college for advanced study was considered not only unnecessary but even a little strange. It *was* a venture into the unknown because all I knew for sure in the beginning was that I wanted to share in the great tasks faced by the colleges. Better education, in both intellectual and spiritual areas, offers an eventual solution to human problems through more accurate thinking and well adjusted personalities.

A college student again. It was twenty years since I had been on a campus full time. Being a full-time college student was different from taking an occasional night course. I was particularly interested in the undergraduates; I admired their quick minds and enthusiasm for the future. One attractive woman majored in journalism. She flashed through quizzes like they were nothing while I sat trying to dredge up obscure facts. I was happy when my scores approached hers. Usually she had a bit of news about "her guy," a senior in pharmacy. Maybe he would not take her out because they had to study, or perhaps she was full of the plans for her marriage in the summer. To her no problem was too great to be capable of solution. She was alert in every respect, a really stimulating person.

Words. With all this English and psychology I learned something about words. Their variations in meanings are more important to communication than I had realized. Semantics proves how elusive a quality meaning can be. Does grass seem to be a simple word, easy to know the meaning? Consider the artist who sees grass in terms of color and form, like Shakespeare, "How lush and lusty the grass looks! How green!" Current slang indicates a horrible meaning for some.

Even that weary feeling will find reflection in the grass, according to Yeats, "Take life easy, as the grass grows on the weirs."

The advertising for a movie implies an unexpected meaning for Wordsworth's lines:

> Nothing can bring back the
> Hour of splendour in the grass,
> Of glory in the flower

Sandburg's poem relates grass to sadness, "I am the grass, I cover all." But recollection of Genesis invokes the majesty of creation, "Let the earth bring forth grass." The fragility of human life before the universe is associated with the words of Isaiah, "Surely the people is grass."

To the homeowner with an oversize lawn, grass finally becomes just something to be cut. To the old man living in one room alone in a city, grass is something which was cool and prickly and wonderful to his bare feet as a boy. His dreams of heaven include long dead family and friends—and vast fields of that boyhood grass. What does grass mean? Does your mind immediately picture the process of photosynthesis, or does the word touch off a reminder of the Biblical injunction:

> All flesh is as grass, and
> All the glory of man as the flower of grass.

Did I make a mistake? Was it wise to take a year off work to prepare for a new career? On the negative side, getting the master's degree was a bigger task than I anticipated. For example, I revised my 110-page thesis completely or partially seven times. My advisor was patient and kind. He realized that I was out of practice in formal English. Thank you, Dr. Stroud.

Job uncertainty and steadily declining savings can be something to consider, especially with two children—one approaching college age and the other approaching high school. We maintained our same standard of living which was good for morale, but cut sharply into investments.

During the months of school I often wished for the security of my old job and the financial strength of my company.

Soon after I finished my courses at Drake, on April 9, 1961, I signed a contract with a Chicago firm to start work September 1 as consultant to colleges in development and business methods, at $12,000 per year. The president assured me that my income would soon exceed that. He was a multimillionaire with a distinguished reputation in fund raising. He had been executive vice-president of one of the best firms in the United States for years. Before that he was in public relations with newspapers and leading corporations. His office, high up in one of Chicago's best buildings, was richly furnished with oriental art and rare books such as Adam Smith's *Wealth of Nations.* His bushy eyebrows, silvered hair, and immaculate grooming all helped create the impression of wealth and distinction. My IBM background and slight acquaintance with the late Thomas J. Watson, Sr., immediately gave us something in common. He had been buying IBM shares all his life and now had 5,000 of them. I felt it a great opportunity to work for such an outstanding man.

His associate also aroused my admiration. He had been a contributing editor of the *Saturday Review Magazine,* a broadcasting director, Voice of America editor-in-chief, professor of English, and from director of a college association. His numerous books were also impressive.

I gave full time to finishing my thesis until my fine job was to start September 1. In about 3-1/2 months, however, we were on vacation at Pilgrim, Michigan, when I received a letter from the Chicago firm suggesting a delay of "one, two or three months." The really ironic part of this was that only the week before I had a telephone call from Dr. Henry Harmon, President of Drake University, whom I particularly hoped to work for. He asked if I would come over to discuss a "very interesting opportunity." That would have been perfect, but I had to say that I was committed to another job. On September 1, however, I reported for work as stated in the contract. The president of the Chicago firm explained that business had been below expectations but encouraged me to believe that in just two weeks he would have good news. Two weeks later, September 16, I talked to the president again on the telephone from nearby Gary, Indiana. "Looks promising," he said. That is the last I heard from him for many years.

The season for hiring college staff was long over. That had been in the spring and summer. I contacted employment agencies and found there were a few jobs open for which I traveled into several states for interviews. The most attractive turned out to be Director of Development at the Kansas City Art Institute. This included fund raising, construction of new buildings and major improvements, public relations, affiliated organizations, alumni, placement, and out-of-town student recruitment.

And so, after quite some journey, I was on my way with a new career. As you have gathered from the previous pages of this book, it has been a rewarding one, personally gratifying and one which has resulted in some good for others. One aspect I have not touched on is my work in later years as a consultant.

The consulting path. Consulting can be as equally rewarding and gratifying as your development career—but remember your first allegiance should be to your employer. When your clients start to take more and more of your time, you will have to choose; it's the only fair thing to do. For what it's worth, I offer some of my consulting experience.

The Menninger Foundation employed consultants and I heard them present earnestly and emphatically what I already knew. Although the courses and seminars had brought me to that level, I realized it was time to rest assured in the confidence of my own expertise. I applied continuing education funds to areas of greater need.

Starting out. Some of my very best work experiences ever were as a consultant. I enjoyed it so much I did not charge enough, a serious deficiency in the view of others in the business. Worse, I did some free consulting—even spent some of my own money. A waste of time. Free advice is often valued at what it cost. Don't do it.

The first consulting fee came in a strange way. I received a phone call from a man I did not know in a small Illinois town I had never heard of. He wanted me to advise a local group on how to raise some money. By chance, I had a trip scheduled to Illinois and would drive through his town about noon. He agreed to assemble his group for lunch and we set a fee for the two-hour discussion. It was an absolutely wonderful experience for me. For the first hour I listened while enjoying my lunch and for the second hour I told them exactly what to do—then my fee was handed to me. I had never been listened to so carefully, except by my Sheltie when we had some misdeed of his to discuss, and they did what I said! It worked so well, the same man called me again for another group.

The Baptist Memorial Hospital in Kansas City, Missouri, asked me in 1975 to help plan a campaign for new buildings. I enjoyed several conferences on Saturdays and Sundays with James Jeffrey, Director of Development. Some years later, I saw Jim again in Kansas City and he said: "Charlie, I want to take you to lunch at the Alameda Plaza. You remember that plan you gave us in 1975? We followed exactly what you said and raised $13 million."

While I found immense satisfaction in some consulting while employed full time, be careful. Development demands too much time and concentration to permit more than a very little moonlighting.

When I retired at age sixty-five, I began two consulting jobs—both perfect, yielding great satisfaction.

I like to do actual work for the client in the field—make calls.

That, along with study of the organization and its purposes is the basis for preparing plans.

This is an example of a very satisfying piece of consulting work. It was for a Catholic hospital where the devotion and spiritual power of the sisters reminded me of The Reverend Theodore M. Hesburgh, C.S.C., president of Notre Dame for over 30 years. Father Hesburgh shared his methods with us in development meetings and I was inspired to hear the enthusiasm with which he described Notre Dame programs. At the University itself I learned how his staff made sure that the prospects on whom he lavished his attention were financially able and had a strong connection with the school. Hesburgh is one of the great fund raisers of our time and this is what he taught me: "Know your project, know your prospect, and show enthusiasm. Your presentation must have drive, power and sparkle." They couldn't say "no" to Father. With inspiration from him and from the sisters, prospects said "yes" to me also. This is what I reported to the board.

I worked part time for six months making major and deferred giving contracts with prospects to provide an assessment of potential. Over $2 million, mostly wills and trusts, may result if someone is hired to do followup. The contacts were discussed in case-by-case detail to show how cultivation plans may be started and continued.

The caring attitude of the hospital staff was emphasized by all who had been patients and this should be the theme of a brochure. The brochure will graphically present why the hospital is special and worthy of support, plans for the future and finances.

Record keeping and other recommendations were included to present a complete plan to launch a comprehensive major gift cultivation. It was realistic since it was based on field contacts all over the United States.

Incidentally, an interesting aspect of this project was that the doctors were very interested in my reports on former patients. While they lacked much from a medical point of view, it reminded the doctors how useful it would be to have an organized and medically sound followup on the results of treatment.

That reminded me that consultants should do the same. Are those beautiful plans implemented? Do they work?

The perfect solution. The best way to do consulting is to be in a position that clients come to you and to operate with practically no overhead. It worked that way for me because the day after I retired from full-time work with the American Cancer Society,

Illinois Division, I started as a consultant with the American Cancer Society, Missouri Division. I was paid for five days per month and did extra work as a volunteer and so continued for seven years until I decided to retire. I didn't just give advice. I called on prospects, improved the mailing list, recruited volunteers, did training, made reports, and thought of myself as a part-time worker. I loved the work and could not imagine anything better. Thanks, Jerry Quick, Tom Baab, and all who made this wonderful experience possible for me.

If you want something bigger than my one-man operation: a glamour consulting firm with beautiful offices, charming secretaries, computers, first class staff, and plenty of advertising—go for it. All you need to start with is a successful development career, stacks of money, an excellent reputation, and plenty of friends who will help you get business. All you have to do is find and keep good clients and your fortune is made.

Chapter 14

MAKE IT REAL—PART TWO

I wish to conclude this book with a tribute to Dr. William C. Menninger, my greatest teacher in fund raising. Dr. Will was my friend and helped in many ways when I was at Baker University learning the business. Later, when I worked for The Menninger Foundation, he taught me a great deal more through the notes he left in the files and through his writings. I call him the Prince of Fund Raising.

I followed up many of the calls Dr. Will had made and that's when I came to fully appreciate this giant among men.

His father, Charles Frederick Menninger, saw that more complete medical care could be provided by physicians in groups. This pioneering idea led to the founding of the Menninger Clinic. Older brother Karl was Dr. Will's mentor and described by him as "the greatest teacher I ever had." The brothers developed the team approach to include physicians, nurses, recreational therapists, occupational therapists, secretaries, and receptionists into a therapeutic team. My wife, Betty, is an example of how far this reaches. She was a receptionist-typist in the Children's Division and was requested to accomplish certain things with patients and parents who got to know her well and developed confidence in her.

The team included Betty and all those in contact with the patient who could help build good personal relationships.

But can we ordinary people learn from such a great man? Yes, I did—and not a day goes by but my life is richer because of his influence.

"You are more mature if you have found a cause in which to invest your time and money for some social good," wrote Dr. William Menninger. "You can achieve an outstanding characteristic of emotional maturity—the ability to find satisfaction in giving." I have often used such quotes from him in proposals with good effect.

Dr. Will taught that everyone has to adopt a mission that is constructive and so big he has to keep working at it. Aren't you working for the same objectives? You want your donor to take on an important cause and to find satisfaction in giving time and money.

Few of us could hope to copy Dr. Will in his roles as physician, national spokesman for mental health, advisor to the president, responsible for the mental health of over eight million men in World War II, president of physician groups, etc. He was invited to speak to twenty-two legislatures and had a part in the National Mental Health Act.

What we can learn is not how he became so famous and influential but why he was such an excellent fund raiser. Dr. Will was president of The Menninger Foundation with many responsibilities, but he always seemed so relaxed with ample time for whomever he was with. We sat together once on a long plane ride to California. Instead of pulling reports out of his briefcase to study, he just leaned back and smiled and had a good visit with me.

He was effective because of the kind of man he was. His character made people believe in him.

Lewis L. Robbins, Medical Director of Hillside Hospital, described him as "always concerned with how to improve things, always striving for his patients, his students, the Foundation and for mankind . . . never discouraged or angry . . . always time for everyone."

Leo Rangell, when president of the American Psychoanalytic Association, called Menninger "the most outstanding distinguished mental hospital in this country." He was amazed that "this most sophisticated" institution should be in the middle of the United States, so far from Vienna. Dr. Will made this an asset by bringing rural American values to the treatment of the mentally ill. In *Memorial for William C. Menninger,* Rangell described him as "big, direct and straightforward, forceful and pragmatic, there was no conflict with American geniality, with the Masons or with the Boy Scouts of America. There was no conflict with deeply held religious convictions."

In *Living in a Troubled World,* Dr. Will wrote that "every religion has taught us that God is love—and that it is from Him that one can gain strength."

Dr. Will, in his visits with people all over the world, mentioned his hopes for The Menninger Foundation and described various programs which obviously needed more funds to carry forward. But his way of operating was more effective than to just sell himself or The Menninger Foundation. He promoted emotional maturity and became famous for his statement on *"The Criteria of Emotional Maturity":*

> The ability to deal constructively with reality.
> The capacity to adapt to change.
> A relative freedom from symptoms that are produced by tensions and anxieties.
> The capacity to find more satisfaction in giving than receiving.
> The capacity to relate to other people in a consistent manner with mutual satisfaction and helpfulness.
> The capacity to sublimate, to direct one's instinctive hostile energy into creative and constructive outlets.
> The capacity to love.
>
> William C. Menninger, M.D.
> 1899–1966

He taught how to accept frustration "with a fair degree of grace." He pointed out that "many of the problems the psychiatrist sees are related to the failure of people to grow." To control anxiety, learn to "live with yourself as you are."

The message which helped most to produce gifts was: "Give of Yourself." He described how much Scout work meant, "something bigger than myself . . . one of the most rewarding corners of my life."

He urged reaching out to help others. Learn caring. "In our capacity to love—caring for our fellow man, wherever he lives—rests much of the solution to world problems today."

Dr. Will encouraged everyone to give time and resources to worthy causes as a step in achieving emotional maturity. He was right. Giving helps the donors.

Promote that and you will be following in the steps of a great man.

Despite Dr. Will's amazing ability to attract gifts to The Menninger Foundation, he could have raised millions more if he had occasionally in a speech or conversation, said, "Remember The Menninger Foundation in your will."

Extend this speculation to imagine how Dr. Will could have magnified his power by:

1. Computers to select prospects, send special mailings, etc.
2. New ways to organize volunteers.
3. Specific and detailed proposals for large sums to persons of great wealth.

4. Imaginative special events and educational programs such as The Menninger Foundation has excelled in since his death in 1966.

The public support built up by the Menningers continues and grows in strength. A letter dated August 25, 1986, from Patrick Burnau, senior vice-president, public affairs, states that eighteen new buildings now stand on the West Campus; the first clinic outside Topeka, in Albuquerque, was opened in 1985 and endowment has quadrupled.

In the last twenty years fund raising has been improved enormously, but in seeking major gifts—remember the power of personal relationships.

Your goal is to combine the magic of great personal magnetism with the best methods.

The reason it is worth your time to consider Dr. Will is that he demonstrated how to persuade against enormous obstacles. Read his speeches in *"A Psychiatrist for a Troubled World."*

People in the first half of this century did not want to think about the insane and the mentally ill. "Forget them! Put them away! We spend too much on them already!"

Dr. Will carried the day against massive apathy. How? (Isn't apathy your biggest problem?)

One example comes from notes on an address he made before the Michigan Legislature in 1956. You can use these same steps (the bulleted italic phrases below) in your presentations and proposals.

- *Identify with Your Audience*

  Dr. Menninger paid tribute to leaders in his field such as brother Karl "who gave the vision and guidance and energy more than any other one person."

- *Positive Approach*

  Why there is "a new era of hope."

- *Tell Something about Yourself*

  How the Clinic was started with his father and brother, four years in the Surgeon General's Office, "worry about the mental health of eight million men" and developing programs for the Veterans' Administration brought him to a tremendous point he often made on the importance of mental health: "Two and a half million men were lost" to the World War II war effort because of emotional problems.

• *Tell a Success Story*

Menninger leadership achieved wonders in the home state of Kansas.

To start with, the Topeka State Hospital had 1,850 patients and "two doctors, one a chronic alcoholic and the other who really had no training." Per diem allotment per patient was $1.06.

The solution was to "buy brains over bricks." In Karl Menninger's words, "Many patients will get well in a barn if you give them the right doctor and the right treatment. We don't want them to live in barns, but staff and treatment come first."

A professional staff was obtained by recruiting and training, salaries increased, the inept replaced. One big help was a grant from The Rockefeller Foundation for training.

"Occupational and recreational programs were started, fire escapes installed, a patients' canteen constructed . . . we developed a very extensive volunteer system." Patients came to believe they could get well.

When qualified doctors began to see patients the population of the hospital dropped 26 percent. Instead of spending millions on new buildings, patients were helped and discharged.

The Menninger style of taking an interest was demonstrated for me when Dr. Karl Menninger came to speak to our Baker University student body.

After the talk I was to escort Dr. Karl to a private dining room for lunch with some trustees. We were late because of the number of questions, so I chose the shortest route, through the cafeteria. As I tried to hurry through, the great man stopped to talk with each student who had asked a question. The students were much more important to him than the trustees or his own lunch. The significance of the latter was made clear to me in later years when I discovered how much Dr. Karl enjoyed food. But he knew how to select priorities.

• *Persuade the Prospect to See for Himself*

Dr. Will "Arranged for every member of the Kansas legislature and his wife to visit the state hospital . . . they saw beds in the halls and the mattresses on the floor at night . . . they saw inadequate and ill-prepared food . . . they saw patients cooped up for days on end . . . they saw physical restraints, straitjackets all over the place, untrained and often uncouth and, I can tell you, brutal attendants." Such visits got things started on this success at his own state hospital.

Your words are not enough. Take your prospect to see what you want improved. It worked for Dr. Will.

The famous Dr. Eli Ginzberg of Columbia University said, "I have never doubted for a moment that one man, William C. Menninger, was the spearhead of one of the most fundamental revolutions in modern American life—the recognition that mental illness, like every other major illness, must be confronted and overcome."

Few of us can be another Will Menninger. What we can do is to practice the art of friend making as he did and be the better for it.

CONCLUSION

Most aspects of development are interesting and enjoyable, but major gift cultivation is the most fun and provides the greatest satisfaction.

Your job is to get money—this way you get more for your time and effort.

And the fringe benefits are terrific—you make friends with people of outstanding accomplishment and of wonderful generosity.

Each major gift is a great achievement for the donor and a heartwarming experience for you. May you have more than I had and love every minute of it.

SECRETS OF MAJOR GIFT FUND RAISING CHAPTER SUMMARY STUDY GUIDES

Chapter 1. MAKE IT REAL—PART ONE

BE A FRIEND because you want to be—not because you want money.

ENJOY WHAT YOU DO, and others will enjoy working with you.

COMMUNICATE APPRECIATION to your prospects and donors for what they have done.

REVIEW CHAPTER 2.

YOUR NOTES:

SECRETS OF MAJOR GIFT FUND RAISING CHAPTER SUMMARY STUDY GUIDES

Chapter 2. CULTIVATE, MOTIVATE, ASK, AND FOLLOW UP

BALANCE the two driving forces of your cultivation

- keep it short and direct *yet*
- make it long range

CULTIVATION IS THE KEY to big gift success.
REMEMBER: Big gifts start small.

MOTIVATE

- have the right words ready
- search for the motivation
- several calls on the same prospect can help
- bring out the motivation
- concentrate on the donor's cause-related needs
- recognize the individual
- learn and listen

THE "CALL"

When making the call:

- establish rapport
- use emotion wisely
- focus on the prospect
- focus on what the prospect needs
- help your prospects make gifts that are good for your organization *and* them
- use the folder or brochure as a means to follow up, not the final opportunity
- make long-range plans as appropriate to the prospect

FRIENDSHIP IS AN IMPORTANT MOTIVATOR

- A great friend makes a great fund raiser.
- Be a friend to be a friend, not just to get a gift.
- Think about how your prospect views you.
- Show interest in what is important to your prospect.

INTERVIEW TIPS

- assume acceptance
- start slow and build up
- tell what the "product" will do for them
- use credit reports wisely to obtain information
- control the interview
- be sensitive; avoid the hard sell Remember: you are a friend helping the prospect make a good gift
- simplify
- be direct
- come to the point

See also Chapter 11.

ASK FOR THE GIFT

- Just following the perfect plan and build-up will never get you a gift; you need to ask!
- Practice asking; then do it! Have those words ready.

FOLLOW UP

- Make only those prospect calls you know you can follow up.
- Regular follow up will get results.
- Match follow-up techniques to the prospect:
  —telephone
  —mail
  —personal call by yourself, volunteer, or other friend
  —invitation to join or participate in

organization as volunteer, committee or board member
—ensure that you do follow up
—use —large appointment book
—monthly tickler files, either manila folders or a computerized version

YOUR NOTES:

SECRETS OF MAJOR GIFT FUND RAISING CHAPTER SUMMARY STUDY GUIDE

Chapter 3. EXPLORE "THE RULES" FOR YOURSELF

EVALUATE the rules of thumb critically and honestly in light of your experiences and changing times. Ask yourself these questions, annually or for each prospect as needed, and provide your *own* answer:

Are tax laws a motivator now, in these times?

Send no more than two persons on this call?

Is an appointment harder to get than the gift?

Can brochures backfire? What printed material is right for this prospect?

Might a tailored proposal be appropriate?

When is the "buy" (giving) decision made?

What are the rewards of giving?

Involve the spouse?

What *does* it take to get and keep a bequest?

What *does* motivate a donor?

Is a million dollar gift possible? Or is a series of major gifts more likely?

YOUR NOTES:

SECRETS OF MAJOR GIFTS
CHAPTER SUMMARY STUDY GUIDE

Chapter 4. MAKE SPEECHES AND SEMINARS PAY OFF

Talk about

- stories of others' satisfaction through giving
- how to turn prospect problems into donor solutions

Plan the seminar well:

Research the prospect lists of potential attendees

Is the seminar going to be promoted adequately?

Seminar checklist:

[ ] topic appeals to family or personal interest
[ ] topic is currently in the news
[ ] seminar site suits your group
[ ] panelists are known to you as experts *and* good presenters
[ ] prospect follow up forms are ready (see fig. 4–1)

Do not underestimate the value of **your reputation;** seminars can build it to where it will be a great help in your calls.

Final tips:

- put your message in a story
- prepare thoroughly
- be part of the audience—remove barriers

YOUR NOTES:

SECRETS OF MAJOR GIFT FUND RAISING CHAPTER SUMMARY STUDY GUIDE

Chapter 5. USE DIRECT MAIL AS A MEANS, NOT AN END

The effective mailing program requires:

- a good list
- effective literature that
  - —personalizes the message
  - —provides information of value to the reader
  - —conveys honesty and integrity
  - —avoids extreme statements
  - —is conversational and pleasant
- appropriate timing
- design that is appropriate for the recipients
- follow up, follow up, follow up

YOUR NOTES:

SECRETS OF MAJOR GIFT FUND RAISING CHAPTER SUMMARY STUDY GUIDE

Chapter 6. BE SENSITIVE TO PROSPECTS' NEEDS

REMEMBER, the older segments of your prospect list often have special needs. When the props of an active life's work have been replaced by the fruits of leisure, a good two-step approach is:

- Hold a general meeting with a group of prospects, followed by
- A personal conference for the decision, in which you
  —use an easel to cut down on paperwork
  —don't talk too fast
  —don't mumble
  —are clear
  —get the decision

OVERCOME THE OBJECTIONS of nonresponsive prospects:

"I need my money for retirement."
Overcome with charitable remainder trust with lifetime income.

"I hate to pay attorneys."
Offer the free services of your volunteer attorney for discussion of possibilities.

"I'm out of money."
Put prospect in touch with volunteer who, in roughly same circumstances, did manage to make a gift.

"I just haven't gotten around to it."
Usually, this is a cover for some other perceived problem with the gift or a fear that the process is terribly complicated. Try to find out what lies behind the statement, then address the issues accordingly.

"The management of the gift is too much of a burden."
If this comes up in relationship to property, explain the benefits of a unitrust. For other types of gifts, what may be at issue is, again, fear of a complex process or a less than full understanding of what exactly is being proposed.

"But there'll be an estate tax. I hate paying taxes!"
Make sure the donor understands how a charitable trust can reduce or avoid the tax burden on the surviving spouse or children before accepting this answer.

BE ALERT to the occasional prospect who will use your offer as an opportunity to solve a personal problem, with no intention of ever making a gift.

SENTIMENT CAN MOTIVATE, but use this tool wisely; don't use it to take unfair advantage of the prospect. Don't count on sentiment alone.

PERSONAL ATTENTION need not be time consuming and can pay great dividends.

YOUR NOTES:

SECRETS OF MAJOR GIFT FUND RAISING CHAPTER SUMMARY STUDY GUIDE

Chapter 7. SEEK THE DEFERRED GIFT

You **CAN** Learn deferred giving

You **NEED NOT** be a legal expert to achieve

YOUR OBJECTIVE: To present the advantages of a deferred gift; *defer* the legal and tax details to a proposal prepared by your attorney.

DEFERRED GIFTS:

- memorialize a life
- provide donor self-fulfillment
- provide unending recognition
- protect income
- confer tax advantages
- make larger than cash gifts possible
- enable relinquishing investment burdens
- are less vulnerable to attack by heirs
- facilitate property control after death through trust provisions
- provide privacy and avoid publicity; will probate does not
- provide a way to make a gift with little or no reduction in income (if this is important)

OBTAIN INFORMATION from the many seminars, courses, and books available. For a partial list of resources, see appendices.

SPECIALIZE IN DEFERRED GIVING

IF: the work appeals to you, you need a new challenge, you want to work with people.

WHEN: others come to you for deferred gift advice.

TIPS FOR THE DEFERRED GIFT SPECIALIST

- Beware of lawyers who see no need to keep up to date on IRS regulations, U.S. Tax Court decisions, and revisions of the tax code
- Qualify your prospects
- Use your volunteer pool
- Interview tips:
  —Pursue your objectives in a relaxed, conversational manner.
  —Take notes.
  —Establish yourself as a future source of information.

YOUR NOTES:

SECRETS OF MAJOR GIFT FUND RAISING CHAPTER SUMMARY STUDY GUIDE

Chapter 8. DON'T BE AFRAID OF REAL ESTATE

TAKE THE GOOD DEAL

- Think saleable, rather than attractive.
- Don't be greedy; be satisfied if just a percentage is your share.
- Beware the occasional con artist.
- If it's too good to be true, check it out thoroughly.
- Avoid property that's been on the market for a long time or is in an area in which others are unlikely to buy.
- Don't refuse the "small" gift; it may appreciate into a much larger one tomorrow.

SEEK THE RIGHT EXPERT HELP

- Use a competent real estate professional.
- Look for a retired professional who may be willing to volunteer.
- Learn and use the right terminology with real estate professionals.

YOUR NOTES:

WAYS TO GET BIG GIFTS
CHAPTER SUMMARY STUDY GUIDE

Chapter 9. DEVELOP THYSELF, DEVELOPMENT DIRECTOR

MANAGE YOUR TIME FOR RESULTS

Use each minute constructively, *but* don't miss a lead to a big gift; answer every inquiry as completely as you can

THE "SELL" must always be a balance of hard facts presented in a soft way and always in good taste.

THEREFORE,

Listen to the voices of experience, yours and others'—and tailor the approach to the prospect

WHO PAYS FOR LUNCH?

- First invitation—you made it, you should pay.
- Second or additional times—you'll probably be invited and should not have to pay. However, be prepared to pay.

USE, DON'T ABUSE, THE TELEPHONE

The telephone is a great tool for building relationships; it is a poor one for the close (how can you offer the pen for signing?).

QUALIFY YOUR PROSPECTS THROUGH MOTIVATION

- Determining if motivation even exists saves you and the prospect time and effort.
- Probe early to discover motivation—or lack thereof—and thus qualify the prospect.
- Develop a style that works with your prospect's deepest motivation: the prospect will then sell himself (or herself) **REREAD CHAPTERS 2 AND 6.**

DEVELOP YOUR LEADERSHIP SKILLS

- **EVALUATE YOUR PERSONAL TOUCH.** Remember why you do what you do. Keep in personal contact with those you serve—allocate 25 percent to 30 percent of your time.
- **EMPHASIZE SERVICE OF YOUR PROSPECTS' AND DONORS' NEEDS.** Evaluate your department's quality of service. Experience it yourself when possible. Through your visits, determine if prospects who have become donors are glad they did; for those who didn't become donors, see if you can find out why.
- **EMPHASIZE HELPING, GOING BEYOND THE CALL OF DUTY.** Impress staff with the need for going out of their way, beyond their job descriptions, to help any of the public they contact—then practice what you preach.
- **RESPOND TO COMPLAINTS.** Complaints are your golden opportunity to make an impression and a friend.
- **LET YOUR STAFF AND DONORS TELL YOU HOW TO DO BETTER.**
  —Ask your staff to follow up with donors; are they happy with what you're doing?
  —Give your donors opportunities to give you feedback.
- **ACKNOWLEDGE CONTRIBUTIONS PUBLICLY.** Nothing motivates staff or prospects more than public acknowledgment of a job well done or gift given.
- **INVOLVE YOUR STAFF—AND YOURSELF.**
  - Meet with your staff—paid and unpaid—on a regular basis.
  - Spend time on the front lines.

- **KNOW YOUR LIMITATIONS—AND YOUR STRENGTHS.**
  —Don't be afraid to use consultants when you need them, but be sure you know when it is worthwhile.
  —Learn enough about the areas of which you know little to determine whether you wish to pursue knowledge and become proficient or are better off leaving it in the hands of the experts.
  —Don't try to become an expert on everything.

UNDERSTAND LEADERSHIP

THE LEADER is not only the president or development director, but anyone who must get others to work, who must get prospects enthused.

GOOD LEADERS must lead by example. They

- provide the dramatic goal and vision.
- make the work fun.
- listen—and speak when needed.
- help others achieve.
- focus their boards of directors on the priority objectives.

REREAD CHAPTER 11.

USE PAPERWORK EFFECTIVELY

GUIDELINES clarify policy and responsibility, help avoid misunderstanding.

REPORTS are necessary to help you and others to measure progress and effectiveness, as well as to promote and encourage communication. They also serve to make others feel involved and aware. They also tell the boss what it is you do.

ACCURATE RECORDS are a must; they'll help you gauge your progress, make future plans, and write your reports.

TRAINING MANUALS, when brief, can be excellent tools for training and serve the same purposes as guidelines.

YOUR NOTES:

SECRETS OF MAJOR GIFT FUND RAISING CHAPTER SUMMARY STUDY GUIDE

Chapter 10. KNOW WHEN TOO MUCH REALLY ISN'T

AVOID THE TWO MYTHS OF BIG GIFT FUND RAISING.

MYTH #1—**Big gift fund raising is more trouble than it is worth.**

(Initially, yes; payoffs come only after about four years. But when they do, they come in big.)

MYTH #2—**Big gift programs cost more money than other forms of fund raising.**

(Over time, big gift fund raising can cost no more than 1.5 cents for every dollar raised.)

YOUR NOTES:

SECRETS OF MAJOR GIFT FUND RAISING CHAPTER SUMMARY STUDY GUIDE

Chapter 11. TELL THE MANAGEMENT STORY—INSPIRE AND MOTIVATE

TELL YOUR PROSPECTS.

Tell prospects how good your management of their funds is—they want to know their gifts are being handled wisely.

TELL YOUR STAFF

Tell your staff (and your boss) how good their management and work is by:

- encouraging innovation
- telling their success stories
- focusing their attention on the primary activity
- avoiding bureaucracy
- letting them prove it to themselves by participating in other areas.

REREAD CHAPTER 9.

YOUR NOTES:

SECRETS OF MAJOR GIFT FUND RAISING CHAPTER SUMMARY STUDY GUIDE

Chapter 12. USE VOLUNTEERS

CREATE A VOLUNTEER SOLICITATION COMMITTEE.

Create a committee of volunteers to target $500+ donors; members should be prominent community citizens and leaders.

Qualifications: solicitation volunteers should

- have annual income comparable to that of prospects
- have influence in the community
- be willing to make a personal contribution or pledge upon becoming involved.
- be willing to cultivate five prospects during the year.

Responsibilities: to develop, in conjunction with staff director

- objectives
- timetable
- publicity
- record-keeping system
- speakers' bureau
- recognition for donors

SELECT THE RIGHT VOLUNTEER

MATCH the volunteer's background and interests to the prospects being solicited.

GET BACKGROUND INFORMATION on potential volunteers before you select, to ensure insofar as possible that the leaders and workers you choose can and will do the job.

TRAIN AND EVALUATE

see fig. 12-1, Suggested Action Plan
fig. 12-2, Achievement Report

YOUR NOTES:

SECRETS OF MAJOR GIFT FUND RAISING
CHAPTER SUMMARY STUDY GUIDE

Chapter 13. **BECOME A SUCCESSFUL FUND RAISER**

STRIVE always to **ACHIEVE** and **STRETCH** yourself **TO THE LIMITS** of **YOUR PROFESSION** and of **YOUR HUMANITY.**

YOUR NOTES ON YOUR CAREER PROGRESS:

YOUR NOTES ON DEALING WITH OTHERS:

SECRETS OF MAJOR GIFT FUND RAISING
CHAPTER SUMMARY STUDY GUIDE

Chapter 14. MAKE IT REAL—PART TWO

BE SINCERE—believe in what you do.
MAKE TIME FOR OTHERS—give of yourself and others will give of themselves.

IDENTIFY with your audience.

BE POSITIVE in your approach.

TELL SOMETHING ABOUT YOURSELF.

TELL THE SUCCESS STORIES OF OTHERS who did it.

INVITE PROSPECTS TO SEE for themselves.

YOUR NOTES TO INSPIRE YOURSELF:

Appendix A

Recent Books

The following list is one of publications I have found useful or have been recommended. Those marked by an asterisk (*) are also available from the Taft Group. Prices and availability are subject to change.

America's Hidden Philanthropic Wealth
The Taft Group
5130 MacArthur Blvd., NW
Washington, DC 20016

America's Wealthiest People
The Taft Group
5130 MacArthur Blvd., NW
Washington, DC 20016
Price: $57.50

The Art of Asking
Paul H. Schneiter
Fund-Raising Institute
Box 365
Ambler, PA 19002-0365
Price: $22.50

Bequests, Endowments & Special Gifts
Richard H. Stough
1981
J L J Publishers

Campus America, September, 1965.
American College Public Relations Assn.
"Motives in Educational Philanthropy" by Irvin G. Wyllie, Chairman, Department of History, University of Wisconsin.
Note: This paperback may be available through CASE. It is not "recent," but has lots of vital ideas.

Capital Ideas
M. Jane Williams
Fund-Raising Institute
Box 365
Ambler, PA 19002-0365
Price: $49.95

The Charitable Giving Service Tax Reference Library
Longman/R & R Newkirk

500 North Dearborn Street
Chicago, IL 60610-4975

Charitable Giving and Solicitation
Stern, Schumacher and Martin
Prentice-Hall Information Services
240 Frisch Court
Paramus, New Jersey 07652

Confessions of a Fund Raiser
Maurice G. Gurin
The Taft Group
5130 MacArthur Blvd., NW
Washington, DC 20016
Price: $24.95

Dear Friend: Mastering the Art of Direct Mail Fund Raising
Kay Partney Lautman and Henry Goldstein
The Taft Group
5130 MacArthur Blvd., NW
Washington, DC 20016
Price: $47.50

Deferred Gifts: How to Get Them
George V. King
Fund-Raising Institute
Box 365
Ambler, PA 19002-0365
Price: $44.95

Designs for Fund-Raising
Harold J. Seymour
Fund-Raising Institute
Box 365
Ambler, PA 19002-0365
Price: $41.50
This book from the 1960s is a classic.

Development Today
Dr. Jeffrey Lant
Lant Associates

Direct Mail Copy That Sells!
Henry Hoke, Jr.
Hoke Communications, Inc.
224 Seventh Street
Garden City, NY 11530
Price: $18.95

The Experts Guide to Generating Major Gifts
Little Brown and Co.
34 Beacon Street
Boston, MA 02106
Price: $60.00

FRI Prospect-Research Resource Directory
1986
Fund-Raising Institute
Box 365
Ambler, PA 19002-0365

Fund Raising: The Guide to Raising Money from Private Sources Second Edition, 1986
Thomas E. Broce
University of Oklahoma Press
1005 Asp Avenue
Norman, OK 73019
Price: $19.95

Giving USA-Annual Report
Giving in 1985
American Association of Fund Raising Counsel
25 W. 43rd Street, Suite 1519
New York, NY 10036
Price: $30.00

How To Build a Big Endowment, 3rd Edition, 1986
Staff of Public Management Institute
358 Brannan Street
San Francisco, CA 94107

How To Find Philanthropic Prospects
1986
Fund-Raising Institute
Box 365
Ambler, PA 19002-0365

How To Help People Give
J. Richard Murray
Development Counsel
P.O. Box 14334
North Palm Beach, FL 33408-0334

How To Hire The Right Fund Raising Consultant
Arthur D. Raybin
The Taft Group

5130 MacArthur Blvd., NW
Washington, DC 20016
Price: $24.95

How to Manage a Non-Profit Organization
John Fisher, INFO, Toronto, Canada
available in the U.S. from:
The Taft Group
5130 MacArthur Blvd., NW
Washington, DC 20016
Price: $22.50

How to Rate Your Development Office
Robert J. Berendt, J. Richard Taft
The Taft Group
5130 MacArthur Blvd., NW
Washington, DC 20016
Price: $21.95

How to Solicit Big Gifts, revised Edition, 1986
Daniel Lynn Conrad
Public Management Institute
358 Brannan Street
San Francisco, CA 94107
Price: $49.00

How To Write Successful Foundation Presentations
Joseph Dermer
The Taft Group
5130 MacArthur Blvd., NW
Washington, DC 20016
Price: $14.00

In Search of Excellence
Thomas J. Peters and Robert H. Waterman, Jr.
1982
Harper & Row, Publishers, New York

Letter Perfect: How To Write Business Letters That Work
Fred Nauheim
Hoke Communications, Inc.
224 7th St.
Garden City, NY 11530
Price: $22.95

Manual: 1986 Tax Reform Act—Analysis and Implications
1986
Pentera, Inc.
8650 Commerce Park Place, Suite G
Indianapolis, IN 46268

Mega Gifts
Jerold Panas
Pluribus Press, Inc., 1984
Division of Teach 'em, Inc.
160 E. Illinois Street
Chicago, IL 60611
Based on thirty interviews with $1 million-and-up donors, one thousand questionnaires from development people. Emphasis on motivation and special characteristics of very large givers.

The Nine Keys to Successful Volunteer Programs
Kathleen Brown Fletcher
The Taft Group
5130 MacArthur Blvd., NW
Washington, DC 20016
Price: $19.95

The Non-Profit Organization Handbook
T. D. Connors
available through:
Hoke Communications, Inc.
224 Seventh Street
Garden City, NY 11530
Price: $59.95

A Passion for Excellence
Thomas J. Peters and Nancy Austin
1985
Random House, NY

People In Philanthropy
The Taft Group
5130 MacArthur Blvd., NW
Washington, DC 20016
Price: $197.00

Philanthropy and Marketing
James Gregory Lord
The Taft Group
5130 MacArthur Blvd., NW
Washington, DC 20016
Price: $47.50

The Planned Gifts Counselor
The Taft Group
5130 MacArthur Blvd., NW
Washington, DC 20016
Price: $87 annually; monthly newsletter

The Planned Giving Deskbook: A Continuing Guide to Tax Law and Charitable Giving
Alden B. Tueller, JD.
The Taft Group
5130 MacArthur Blvd, NW
Washington, DC 20016
Price $94.95

Planned Giving Ideas
Virginia L. and Garigan Carter
1980
CASE

Playing The Funding Game
Gregory C. Horgen
Hoke Communications, Inc.
224 Seventh Street
Garden City, NY 11530
Price: $24.95

The Proposal Writer's Swipe File
The Taft Group
5130 MacArthur Blvd., NW
Washington, DC 20016
Price: $18.95

Prospecting: Searching Out The Philanthropic Dollar
The Taft Group
5130 MacArthur Blvd., NW
Washington, DC 20016
Price: $23.95

The Successful Small Agency—500 Ways to Raise Money*
Phillip T. Drotning

There's Plenty* (Of Money For Non-Profit Groups Willing To Earn Their Shares)
J. H. Prichard
Price $57.00

The Thirteen Most Common Fund-Raising Mistakes and How To Avoid Them
Paul H. Schneiter and Donald T. Nelson
The Taft Group
5130 MacArthur Blvd., NW
Washington, DC 20016
Price: $19.95

Trustees and The Future of Foundations
John W. Nason
Hoke Communications, Inc.
224 Seventh Street
Garden City, NY 11530
Price: $4.95

Where the Money Is: A Fund Raiser's Guide to the Rich
Helen Bergan
1985
Bio Guide Press
P.O. Box 16072-B
Alexandria, VA 22302

Appendix B

Selected Sources of Information

This is a list of those companies with which I've had some dealings and been well pleased with the result. It is not comprehensive, and there are many other firms available who no doubt do just as good work.

American Association of Fund Raising Counsel (AAFRC)
25 W. 43rd Street, Suite 1519
New York, NY 10036

CASE—Council for Advancement and Support of Education
11 Dupont Circle, Suite 400
Washington, DC 20036

National Society of Fund Raising Executives (NSFRE)
1101 King St., Suite 3000
Alexandria, VA 22314

Resource Development, Inc.
Three Corporate Square
Suite 3-100
1949 E. Sunshine
Springfield, MO 65804

John F. Rich Company
One Franklin Plaza
Philadelphia, PA 19102

R. & R. Newkirk
P.O. Box 1727
Indianapolis, IN 46206

Robert F. Sharpe & Company, Inc.
5050 Poplar Avenue
Memphis, TN 38157

The Taft Group
5125 MacArthur Blvd., NW
Washington, DC 20016

(Taft offers newsletters such as "Corporate Giving Watch," "The Taft Foundation Reporter," and "Foundation Giving Watch," as well as fund-raising donor directories and how-to books.)

Marts & Lundy, Inc.
Meadowlands Corp. Cntr.

1200 Wall Street, West
Lynhurst, NJ 07071

The Pentera Group, Inc.
6068 No. Keystone
Indianapolis, IN 46220

Philanthropy Tax Institute
Taxwise Giving
Conrad Teitell
Phone: 203/637-4553
13 Arcadia Road
Old Greenwich, CT 06870

Appendix C

Selected Consultants

Again, this is a list of firms with which I've had good experience. It is not comprehensive, and there are many other firms available who no doubt do work just as good. The AAFRC (American Association of Fund-Raising Counsel) and the NSFRE (National Society of Fund Raising Executives) are good resources of consulting individuals and firms (see Appendix B).

American City Bureau
9501 West Devon Avenue
Rosemont, IL 60018-4879

Campbell & Company
One East Wacker Drive
Chicago, IL 60601

Cargill Associates
Fund Raising Services
4701 Altamesa Blvd.
Box 330339
Fort Worth, TX 76163-0339

Crescendo Planned Gifts Marketing Software
Comdel, Inc.
Golden Pacific Plaza
1601 Carmen Drive
Camarillo, CA 93010

Donnelley Marketing
A Company of The Dun & Bradstreet Corporation
1515 Summer St.
P.O. Box 10250
Stamford, CT 06804

Haney Associates, Inc.
1021 East Las Olas Blvd.
Fort Lauderdale, FL 33301

Hoke Communications, Inc.
224 7th Street
Garden City, NY 11530

Kennedy Sinclaire, Inc.
810 Belmont Avenue

Post Office Box 8304
North Haledon, NJ 07538-0304

Ketchum, Inc.
Chatham Center
Pittsburgh, PA 15219